Psychotherapy
and the
Spiritual Quest

Psychotherapy and the Spiritual Quest

David G. Benner

BAKER BOOK HOUSE
Grand Rapids, Michigan 49516

Copyright 1988 by
Baker Book House Company

ISBN: 0-8010-0948-0

Printed in the United States of America

Library of Congress Cataloging-in-Publication Data

Benner, David G.
   Psychotherapy and the spiritual quest / David G. Benner.
      p.   cm.
   Bibliography: p.
   Includes index.
   ISBN 0-8010-0948-0
   1. Christianity—Psychology.   2. Psychotherapy—Religious aspects—
Christianity.   3. Spiritual life.   I. Title.
   BR110.B42 1988   74405
   261.5'15—dc19   87-37586
                                                          CIP

To **Juliet,**
for sharing her life
and her love
as my soul friend

Contents

Acknowledgments

A book never reflects only the ideas of its author. While I take responsibility for what is written, a great many people have played a crucial role in shaping this book.

Although I had long been interested in relating my Christian faith to the practice of psychotherapy, the opportunity to work with Tom Andrews, M.D., in developing an eating disorders unit at Glendale Heights Community Hospital in the western suburbs of Chicago in 1983 did more to inspire this book than any other experience. As we struggled to plan, staff, and run a psychiatric treatment program that was responsive to the spiritual dimensions of functioning while providing responsible psychotherapeutic and medical treatment, many of the ideas discussed in these pages first came to be formulated. The ensuing years of work together taught both of us about the ways in which spiritual and psychological aspects of human functioning are inextricably related, and I express deep gratitude to Tom for inviting me to join him in that work.

Ideas born out of experience demand careful reflection before they are committed to paper, and I have been most fortunate to have a ready forum for doing just that. My graduate students in the clinical psychology program at

Wheaton College have been a rich source of stimulation and encouragement as my ideas have been tested and refined in the fire of interaction with them for the past ten years.

Another group who has played a crucial role in shaping this book are my patients. I have learned a great deal from the men and women who have entered psychotherapy with me and courageously struggled to gain freedom and vitality in life. Several of them are presented in these pages, appropriately disguised so as to preserve confidentiality. Many more have not had their stories told. I thank them all for sharing their lives with me and enriching my understanding of persons and of life itself.

I also wish to acknowledge with thanks the contributions made by my colleagues. Many hours of stimulating discussion with a number of psychologists and psychiatrists and with several fine theologians, philosophers, and historians have greatly aided me in clarifying my thinking. Particular thanks go to Drs. Hendrika Vande Kemp, Mark Noll, Peter Toon, Robert Roberts, John Finch, C. Stephen Evans, C. Markham Berry, Charles Carlson, and James Beck for reading earlier versions of this manuscript and offering helpful suggestions for its improvement.

I wish to thank the administration of Wheaton College for providing me with a sabbatical leave during the fall semester of 1986, which allowed me to complete much of the writing of this book. I also thank my graduate assistant Jonathan Feather for his research support. And finally, my thanks to Sean Benner, who has once again shared his dad with a book project, but who has done so with the good humor that is so characteristic of him.

1

Psychotherapy as Soul Care

A Jewish psychiatrist friend recently told me of the tensions that developed in his relationship with his father when he decided to pursue a residency in psychiatry. His father, an Orthodox Jew, had supported him enthusiastically during medical school. However, upon hearing of his son's decision to become a psychiatrist, his father exclaimed, "Why psychiatry? You have the Scriptures. What more do you need for those kinds of problems?"

My friend's father was expressing the opinion that the contemporary practice of psychiatry has much more in common with religion than with medicine or science. These are fighting words to most psychiatrists, who are interested in distancing their profession as far as possible from religion. They view psychotherapy as medical treatment similar to other standard medical procedures, and the psychiatrist as a physician of the mind. However, other health care professionals hold that psychiatry is only tangentially related to medicine. Szasz observes:

> Medical psychotherapists, having had a medical training, only look like other doctors—just as hysterics only look like organically sick persons. The difference between the purely communicational interventions of the psychotherapist and the physiochemical interventions of the

11

physician represents an instrumental gulf between the two
groups that no institutional resemblance can convincingly
close. . . . The medical aspects of psychotherapy are about
as substantial as the legendary emperor's cloak. (Szasz
1961, 306–7)

A similar situation exists in clinical psychology. Since
its inception a century ago, psychology has worked with
diligence to distance itself from both religion and philosophy. Psychologists tend to view religion as prescientific
and therefore as having nothing to do with psychology.
Philosophy, which actually was the source of modern psychology, is viewed by psychologists as inappropriately
speculative and metaphysical, qualities which are judged
to keep philosophers from making significant headway on
the questions of human nature and functioning.

However, while psychologists proudly view their discipline as science, and in fact, the flagship of the natural
sciences, it is quite clear that it is at least as much art as
science. Practicing clinicians have not been able to wait for
the discoveries of their research colleagues. The pressing
problems encountered in clinical practice have moved clinicians more and more beyond merely applying scientifically verified psychological principles and procedures.
These developments have frequently put clinical psychologists in a state of tension relative to academic psychologists, a tension much like that faced by psychiatrists in
relation to other medical specialists.

Changing Definitions of Psychotherapy

Is psychotherapy a medical act or does it belong within
some other framework? The first use of the term *psychotherapy* was in the late nineteenth century; it described
the treatment of disease by psychic (i.e., hypnotic or sug-
gestive) means. Baldwin's *Dictionary of Philosophy and
Psychology* notes that this early use of the term implied
that the *goal* of psychotherapy was changes in bodily

states; only the *method* was psychological (Baldwin 1957, 394). Early psychotherapy was, therefore, psychosomatic medicine.

However, as hypnotism and suggestion came under suspicion at the turn of the century, psychotherapy was left without a broad definitional base. Ellenberger suggests that it was at this juncture that psychotherapy came to be defined as "mind cure" or "mental healing" (Ellenberger 1970). Over the next several decades definitions of psychotherapy increasingly emphasized both psychological methods and psychological goals, that is, the use of psychological methods to bring about the cure of the mind.

The confusion over just what psychotherapy is has not been confined to the competing claims of psychology and medicine. Practitioners of psychotherapy within the Emmanuel Movement of early twentieth-century New England argued that psychotherapy should involve healing through the use of mental, moral, and spiritual methods (Cabot 1908, 5). This position was also espoused in the *Journal of Psychotherapy as a Religious Process*, a publication of the Institute for Rankian Psychoanalysis in Dayton, Ohio, from 1954 to 1956. William Rickel, the journal's editor, wrote in the first issue that the bold assertion of the journal's title was justified by the etymology of the word *psychotherapy*. He argued that because *psychē* means "soul," and *therapist* means "servant," the psychotherapist is therefore a servant of the soul (Rickel 1954, 97). The connection of psychotherapy with the long-standing religious tradition of the cure and care of souls provides strong support for the legitimacy of calling psychotherapy a religious or spiritual process.

Contemporary definitions of psychotherapy, however, emphasize its psychological nature. Allan Bergin's definition is typical in this regard. He says psychotherapy is "any of a variety of psychological means used to modify mental, emotional, and behavioral disorders" (Bergin 1979, 886). However, the actual practice of psychotherapy makes it less clear just exactly what is meant by the term *psychological*. In order to demonstrate this, let us consider two typical cases.

Case Study #1

Joan, a twenty-nine-year-old attorney, was experiencing feelings of unfulfillment and dissatisfaction in her life. She had experienced occasional periods of depression, although they were never so severe that anyone except her husband was aware of them. She also reported growing boredom with her marriage. It was not that there was much conflict. In fact, she said that more conflict might make the relationship more interesting. Rather, the marriage had become dull, and she was wondering if her dissatisfaction with it was the cause of her general unhappiness.

Joan's therapist diagnosed her as having a *dysthymic disorder*, the current term for what used to be called a "depressive neurosis." This diagnosis allowed Joan to receive insurance coverage for her therapy, as it could thus be classified as treatment of a mental disorder. Therapy consisted of helping her explore the dissatisfactions in her life and identify what she wanted to change. Through this process Joan concluded that she had outgrown her marriage and that it was holding her back from further personal and professional development. She terminated therapy a few months after her divorce and reported feeling much better about herself.

How can we best understand Joan's situation? Prior to the present century most people would have thought Joan's problem was spiritual. Her questions related to the purpose and meaning of life and what she should do in order to experience the most fulfillment. She was seeking guidance in making important life decisions, and although she might have resisted direct suggestions, she was clearly looking for help in making these decisions. She may even have known what she wanted to do before seeing the therapist, in which case she would be looking for approval of the plan of action she was considering. Whichever was the case, her dilemma involved questions and decisions that would once have been judged to be spiritual in nature.

Once Joan's problems were identified as a dysthymic disorder, her search for personal fulfillment was interpreted as symptomatic of a mental disorder. Within this framework the real problem was her depression, which presumably lay behind her questions about life. The modification of her life circumstances was thus a part of treatment.

This analysis of Joan's problem and of her treatment is not meant to be a critique of the therapy she received. Nor is it to suggest that her problems were not serious nor of a type for which a psychotherapist's help would be inappropriate. Rather, it is to raise the question of whether her problems were manifestations of a mental disorder. If they were, her psychotherapy was an appropriate application of select principles and techniques of psychological treatment. However, if we perceive her problems as spiritual ones, then we need an alternate way of viewing her therapy.

Case Study #2

Ralph was a forty-six-year-old insurance salesman who sought therapy because of his anxiety and low self-esteem. Most people who knew him professionally saw only his self-confidence and his social graces. These traits were part of what had allowed him to become as successful as he had in sales. However, behind this exterior Ralph felt anxious and unsure of himself. In fact, he reported to his therapist that he was finding it increasingly hard to make sales contacts, and that recently he found himself making excuses to avoid dealing with some people. He also reported that he had few personal friends, indicating that dealing with people all day long on the job made him prefer to be alone when not at work.

Ralph's therapist diagnosed his problem as a generalized anxiety disorder with a possible secondary diagnosis of avoidant personality disorder. These diagnoses describe a pattern of pervasive anxiety within an overall personality style characterized by social withdrawal, low self-esteem, strong needs for affection and acceptance, and a hypersensitivity to rejection. Given these personality traits, it is somewhat surprising that Ralph chose sales as a vocation. When he was questioned about this it became clear that Ralph used sales as compensatory strategy. He longed for involvement with people and felt that if he took a job that forced such involvement, he might come to be more comfortable with people. However, while he was able to play a role that allowed him a degree of vocational success, he remained basically uncomfortable with and afraid of people.

Few people would argue that Ralph did not have a psychological problem. His problems seem to have been appropriately described by his diagnoses. Within current diagnostic nomenclature it is, therefore, also appropriate to describe him as having a mental disorder. However, is it possible that Ralph's problems may be viewed with equal validity as spiritual ones? Could it be that both Ralph's need for affection and his equally strong fear of rejection reflect an underlying spiritual need, possibly a longing to move beyond his self-encapsulation and fear of surrender? Could we see him not merely as a bundle of intrapsychic forces but as a person responding to stirrings within his spirit, albeit within the context of his psychological situation? If so, Ralph may need more than treatment of a mental disorder. He may also need spiritual help.

Historian Judith Neaman argues that the mental health professions have moved from the treatment of the mentally ill to the aid of people with spiritual struggles (Neaman 1975). Carl Jung makes the same point. In *Modern Man in Search of a Soul* he notes that "patients force the psychotherapist into the role of the priest and expect and demand that he shall free them from distress. That is why we psychotherapists must occupy ourselves with problems which strictly speaking belong to the theologian" (Jung 1933, 278). The question is, therefore, how best to understand psychotherapy. Is it the application of scientifically verified medical or psychological procedures, or is it a spiritual or religious activity? As already mentioned, some support for the latter possibility is found in the fact that the historical roots of modern psychotherapy lie in religious soul care practices. Such a historical analysis does not tell us definitively that psychotherapy is a religious or spiritual procedure, or that it is not a medical or psychological one. It does, however, indicate that psychotherapy occupies a domain very close to, if not identical with, that traditionally held by religion.

Physicians of the Soul

It is tempting for psychotherapists to think of their discipline as a new one, describing it as a procedure developed within the last century. The reference point for such dating is usually the work of Sigmund Freud, who is regarded as the founder of psychotherapy. While advocates of such an interpretation may acknowledge some continuity between psychotherapy and the earlier use of verbal methods to change behavior, modern psychotherapy is generally thought to be quite discontinuous with such primitive practices.

One of the problems created by this interpretation of the history of psychotherapy is that it raises the question of how people functioned as well as they did prior to the advent of modern psychotherapy. If, as is commonly suggested, 25 percent of the population require psychotherapy at any given point in time (Strole et al. 1962), how did people cope without psychiatrists and psychologists? The answer is, of course, that they had other people with whom they could talk. Family, friends, and clergy or other

physicians of the soul filled the role usually occupied today by psychotherapists.

Rhetoric as Soul Care

In *The Therapy of the Word in Classical Antiquity* Pedro
Lain Entralgo traces the earliest roots of contemporary
psychotherapy to the ancient Greek rhetoricians (Entralgo
1970). Plato first noted that the task of the physician of the
body is to heal through physical means, whereas the task
of the physician of the soul is to heal through verbal
means. Plato viewed rhetoric as the charm of carefully
chosen words, and in describing their healing power for
maladies of the soul he even recognized the crucial value
of catharsis in soul care.

None of the ancient Greek rhetoricians surpassed Socrates in his clarity of vision and fervor of activity as a physician of souls. Socrates called himself a "healer of the
soul," and it is from the Greek *iatros tēs psychēs* that we
derive the English word *psychiatrist*. In the *Apology* Socrates testifies that, having survived the dangers of war in his
youth, he was set apart by God for the life of philosophy.
But this was no ivory-tower academic profession. In describing his life he states that "[I] spend all my time going
about trying to persuade you, young and old, to make your
first and chief concern not for your bodies nor for your
possessions, but for the highest welfare of your souls"
(Szasz 1978, 28). By means of relentless probing and a mas-
terful use of dialectic reasoning Socrates led people
toward a state of readiness for soul guidance.

The Greek physician of the soul had only one tool, his
words. The "therapy of the word" was the studied use of
words to persuade, challenge, and guide people toward the
goal of perfection (Weaver 1953, 25). While few if any contemporary psychotherapists would be prepared to describe their goal as the perfection of their patients, this
definition places the Greek idea of soul care within the domain occupied today by psychotherapy.

Soul Care in Christianity

Apart from the Greeks and early Romans, who viewed the philosopher as the physician of the soul, most cultures have, until the present, made soul care a religious specialization. Indeed, the history of soul care reveals the presence of such a function from ancient Semitic cultures down to the present (Leech 1977). Each culture and each religion has defined and implemented this care in slightly different ways; however, in each case it has involved "the sustaining and curative treatment of persons in those matters that reach beyond the requirements of the animal life" (McNeill 1951, vii).

Soul care in Christianity had its origins in the practices of the wise men of ancient Israel. The wise men occupied one of the three classes of religious experts (the other two being the priests and the prophets) and were most closely associated with the care of the soul. Wise men counseled their fellows on the principles of the good life and the details of personal conduct. While the prophets concentrated on men's emotions to arouse repentance, wise men relied more upon argument and reasoned admonition. In *The History of the Cure of Souls* McNeill describes them as "practical counselors of souls, proclaiming reverence for God and justice to men, and making plain the path of right conduct" (1951, 9). Rabbis later replaced the wise men as spiritual guides within the Jewish community.

One of the most powerful biblical images of one who cares for the souls of others is that of the shepherd. The Old Testament prophet Ezekiel presents the shepherd as one who feeds the hungry, protects and heals the sick, binds up the broken, and seeks out and finds the lost (Ezek. 34:3–16). When the soul shepherds appointed by God did not adequately carry out their responsibilities, God said he would feed his flock (Ezek. 34:15), carry the young lambs in his bosom (Isa. 40:11), and gently lead people to places of rest and nourishment (Ps. 23:2). In the New Testament, Christ is presented as the good shepherd who gives his life for the sheep and who is their guide and protector (John 10:11–16).

Two components have always been central to soul care in Christianity: the provision of remedy for sin, and assistance in spiritual growth. These are sometimes identified as *soul cure* and *soul care*, respectively. The Latin word *cura* can be translated as either "cure" or "care," and Christian spiritual guidance involves both meanings.

Although sin has been understood in different ways in the major Christian traditions, its remedy in soul care has usually centered around confession and repentance. Roman Catholics have focused principally on specific sins, beginning with recollection of them and moving toward their enumeration in the confessional. When Luther published his criticisms of Roman Catholicism (1520), he acknowledged some value in the enumeration and contemplation of specific sins, but placed more emphasis on acknowledgment of one's sinfulness as a condition of heart (Luther 1960, 210). He called sinfulness the "curvature of the self in upon the self," this leading to an incapacity to trust God. Puritans, Lutheran Pietists, and Calvinist Revivalists continued this emphasis, concerned about the "feeling" of repentance and the "experience" of forgiveness and rebirth. This more experiential approach to dealing with sin has since been a dominant element in many Protestant denominations.

The second concern of Christian soul care has been spiritual development. This has often meant movement through a series of stages from depravity to holiness. While discussion of stages of spiritual development is frequently associated with Roman Catholic theology, in fact such a developmental perspective on the spiritual life has had an important place within Protestantism as well. Its pinnacle is seen in the Puritan theologians. In the sixteenth century, William Perkins detailed ten stages of spiritual growth, and other Puritans continued his efforts. However, regardless of the particular theory of spiritual development, Christian soul care has usually sought to move people toward spiritual maturity by aiding their progress through stages of the spiritual life.

In the history of the care of souls Jesus Christ occupies a unique place. As presented in the synoptic Gospels, his primary method of soul care was dialogue. Jesus strove to lead people toward repentance and a conversion that would flow out of the heart into every sphere of life. His was a message of salvation, of new and abundant life. He proclaimed this message to all who would listen, both through his words and through his life. Verbal instruction was certainly present. However, his frequently indirect and even paradoxical methods of teaching, such as his use of parables, indicated that he was looking not simply for cognitive assent to his teaching but for a total reorientation of life.

Jesus' approach to soul care was based upon his conviction of the immense worth of persons. The importance of the conversion of even one individual is the theme of Christ's parables in Luke 15. Here he presents the great happiness associated with redemption: the joy of the shepherd on the recovery of the one lost sheep, the gladness of the woman who found her one lost coin, and the rejoicing of the angels in heaven over the one sinner who repents. Jesus emphasizes the importance of the soul when he asserts that it is better to be weighted with a millstone and dropped into the sea than to cause one young convert to sin (Mark 9:42).

McNeill suggests that Jesus presents us with two great gifts that are the objects of our deepest strivings: spiritual renewal and spiritual repose (McNeill 1951, 77). Spiritual renewal comes in the new birth, a concept at the very heart of Jesus' teaching. He provides us with the possibility of a new beginning that is so radical and complete that it can be best characterized as a "birth." The gift of spiritual repose he describes as rest for the souls of those who labor and are heavy laden (Matt 11:28–30). Toil is not abolished; rather, Jesus offers to replace a heavy yoke with a light one and to provide restored strength for the task at hand.

The Christian church has, since the time of Christ, made the care and cure of souls one of its primary concerns. We see this as early as the first century A.D., where letters of spiritual guidance, comparable to those later employed by Luther and the other Reformers as their primary tools of soul care, are preserved for us in the New Testament. They reflect the desire of the early Christians to guide the spiritual development of others who sought to follow Christ.

The first evidence of soul care on any sizable scale appears among the desert fathers in Egypt, Syria, and Palestine in the fourth and fifth centuries A.D. Disciples would seek out these holy men for aid in increasing personal holiness. The desert fathers emphasized the dangers of traveling the spiritual road without a guide. But their leadership was not authoritarian; spiritual fathers taught first by example and only secondly by word. Two great representatives of this tradition were Evagrius Ponticus (A.D. 345–399) and John Cassian (A.D. 360–435).

The Eastern Orthodox tradition also esteemed the role of the spiritual guide. The seventh-century guide Dorotheos states in his *Directions on Spiritual Training* that "no men are more unfortunate or nearer perdition than those who have no teachers on the way to God" (Leech 1977, 44). This sentiment is echoed by St. Simeon in the eleventh century, who held that "it is impossible for anyone to learn by himself the art of virtue" (Leech 1977, 45), and so he urged those seeking spiritual growth to find a spiritual guide. The language of the "learning of virtue" is very similar to the view of soul care held by the Greek rhetoricians and philosophers. In fact, one of the earliest articulations of the view that soul healing requires the involvement of another person is found in the writings of the Roman philosopher Cicero (106–43 B.C.), who stated that "the soul that is sick cannot rightly prescribe for itself, except by following the instruction of wise men" (McNeill 1951, 27).

By the fifteenth century the tradition of spiritual direction, or soul care, had spread to Russia, where the spiritual guide was the *startsy* ("old man"). The *startsy* took as his role model Christ the good shepherd. The primary function of the good shepherd was his willingness to suffer for and along with the sheep. Consequently the *startsy* had to be one who had the ability to love others and to make the suffering of others his own. This notion of vicarious suffering on the part of the physician of the soul has tremendous implications for psychotherapy when the *startsy* is recognized as a precursor of the modern therapist. The psychotherapist cannot remain aloof from the suffering of his or her patient. Rather, the therapist must incarnate himself or herself, and entering into the very heart of the patient's chaos and suffering must often vicariously experience and absorb that suffering (Benner 1983).

While the earliest spiritual guides tended to be clergy and often were monks, over time more and more of those filling this office in the pre-Reformation church of the West were laity. In the Celtic church in Great Britain several of the most famous spiritual guides were women. Similarly, in the thirteenth century the Dominicans involved nuns in the task of spiritual guidance. The qualifications remained the same; guides were to be persons of insight and discernment who had made progress in their own spiritual pilgrimage and who could lovingly lead others in spiritual growth.

The practice of spiritual guidance has not received much attention in the Protestant tradition. Leech suggests that this is due to Protestants' suspicion of acts that seem to undermine the place of Christ as the only mediator between persons and God (Leech 1977, 84). This de-emphasis was, however, not intended by the early Reformers. Luther was personally involved in a ministry of spiritual direction with a number of individuals, and his *Letters of Spiritual Counsel* (1955) remains a classic in spiritual literature. Zwingli, while recommending confession to God alone, said that it was appropriate to consult a wise Christian counselor for assistance in spiritual matters (Leech 1977,

85). Calvin also served as a spiritual guide to a number of people. While he stressed that the individual Christian's subservience should only be to God, he saw an important role for the spiritual guide.

Developments in seventeenth-century Pietism and Puritanism also make clear that the Reformation did not abolish the role of the spiritual guide. Philipp Jakob Spener, known as the father of Pietism, conducted such a far-flung correspondence of spiritual counsel that he came to be called the spiritual counselor of Germany. Similarly, the writings of Puritans such as William Perkins (*The Whole Treatise of Cases of Conscience*, 1602), Immanuel Bourne (*The Godly Man's Guide*, 1620), and Richard Baxter (*The Christian Directory*, 1673) all clearly illustrate the important place that spiritual guidance had in Puritanism.

Anglicanism has retained a lively interest in spiritual guidance. Some of the most important writings from this tradition have been William Cunningham's *The Cure of Souls* (1908), Reginald Sommerset Ward's *Following the Way* (1925) and *The Way in Prayer* (1932), and Gilbert Shaw's *The Face of Love* (1959). Two of the most popular current books on spiritual guidance, Tilden Edwards's *Spiritual Friend* (1980) and Kenneth Leech's *Soul Friend* (1977), also grow out of Anglicanism.

From Cure of Souls to Cure of Minds

We have seen that the cure and care of souls has historically been at the very heart of Christianity, and that prior to this it had an important place in Judaism. It is also interesting to note that although the religious roots of psychotherapy are frequently overlooked by contemporary psychotherapists, Freud and other first-generation psychotherapists were aware of the continuity of their procedures with religious soul care. Noting that essential similarity, Freud described psychoanalysis as "pastoral work in the best sense of the words" (Freud 1926, 256). But this similarity was quickly forgotten as psychotherapy came to displace soul care and as the focus of cure moved from the soul to the mind. Let us look more closely at how this came about.

Displacement of Soul Care

It should be noted that changes occurring in spiritual guidance, both within Catholicism and Protestantism, served to pave the way for this transition. The practice of spiritual guidance peaked in the fourteenth and fifteenth centuries and subsequently went into a period of decline. After the Council of Trent (1545–1563) the Catholic practice of soul care experienced a severe narrowing of focus, becoming principally concerned with decisions about religious vocations. Spiritual guides increasingly took as their primary role the guardianship of orthodoxy, and their major preoccupation became the avoidance of heresy and dubious forms of mysticism.

Protestants were changing their understanding and practice of the care of souls in even more radical ways. This was largely due to their emphasis on the priesthood of all believers and the central place of the Bible in personal salvation and spiritual growth. The method of caring for souls that increasingly came to be accepted by the Protestants is illustrated in the writings of Martin Bucer, whose book *On the True Care of Souls* appeared in 1538. Basing his understanding of soul care on Ezekiel 34:16, Bucer argued that the duty of all Christians to each other is "to draw to Christ those who are alienated; to lead back those who have been drawn away; to secure amendment of life in those who fall into sin; to strengthen weak and sickly Christians; to preserve Christians who are whole and strong, and urge them forward in all good" (McNeill 1951, 178). Protestants frequently described these activities as "shepherding" in order to distinguish them from the soul care practiced by Roman Catholics, this being associated with discipline and authority. In contrast, the shepherd was to be gentle, sensitive, and tender—his was an office of love and concern, not one of authority.

The Quakers in the seventeenth century initiated a form of mutual admonition and guidance. This came to replace personal and individualized soul care in other Protestant groups as well. Wesley only rarely spoke or wrote of the care or cure of souls, and when he did he referred to preaching. Once again this reflects the central place of the Word in the Protestant understanding of soul care. The stress in Wesleyan and, later, Holiness churches was on the direct action of God in the life of the individual; consistent with this, spiritual guidance was de-emphasized.

Several prominent Catholic writers also questioned the necessity of spiritual guidance. James Walsh, a Jesuit, argues that spiritual direction "becomes useful and necessary only when the individual who is living the life of the Christian community to its fullest extent possible becomes aware of God's special call to perfection" (Leech 1977, 77). Spiritual guidance is only for the few and is only to be practiced by specialists. Such specialists should not merely possess the personal characteristics long associated with the office, but should also receive specialized training. This professionalization of soul care is clearly related to its movement toward psychotherapy.

Associated with this was the rise of pastoral counseling. In his *History of Pastoral Care in America* Holifield states that the transformation of the cure of souls into pastoral counseling or psychotherapy began in America in 1905 among a group of Episcopalians at the Emmanuel Church in Boston (Holifield 1983, 201). Rector of Emmanuel Church Elwood Worcester and his associate Samuel McComb asked whether the care of souls would continue to be guided by tradition or by the science of psychotherapy. Their recommendation was clearly that it was time for the church to embrace science. What came to be known as the Emmanuel Movement soon attracted support from Congregationalists, Presbyterians, and some Baptists, and within three years the group had its own journal, *Psychotherapy*. Holifield calls this the beginning of the movement from saving souls to supporting self-realization.

Holifield argues that pastoral counseling was an important force in the development of America's therapeutic culture. In fact, he says that the reason America was so ripe for psychotherapy as a new method of soul care was that America's early history was heavily influenced by Pietism. Historically, Pietism and Puritan variations of it have involved a subjective psychological focus on interior experiences. This spiritual introspection, what Holifield calls a "preoccupation with inwardness, rebirth, conversion, [and] revival" (Holifield 1983, 356), was basic to American consciousness. It was, therefore, only a small step to translate introspective spiritual piety into secular psychological piety, and the evolution of pastoral counseling and psychotherapy in the early twentieth century was a major force in this movement.

Great Britain also saw the beginning of interest in psychotherapy as a cure of souls during this same period. The Guild of Pastoral Psychology, of which Jung was president, and the Institute of Religion and Medicine were both committed to building bridges between psychology and theology. Subsequently, the Clinical Theology Association under the leadership of psychiatrist Frank Lake came into being as an organization providing training in pastoral counseling in Great Britain.

But unquestionably the most significant force in the movement of soul care from religion to medicine and psychology was the seventeenth- and eighteenth-century growth of science and the subsequent nineteenth-century decline of religion. Ehrenwald describes the demise of religious soul cure as occurring "when magic has been eroded by critical reason, and religion, emptied of its meaning, has become a formalized institution, a repository of magic rituals and observances" (Ehrenwald 1966, 10). He goes on to say that psychotherapy arose as a stop-gap effort to fill the spiritual void left by the demise of religion. Its challenge was "to meet unmet metaphysical needs ... without recourse to mythical ideologies or magic ritual" (1966, 16).

The great hope of science, particularly the social sciences, was for new solutions to old problems without the outdated trappings of religion. With faces toward the future, modern persons strode ahead with the confidence that myth and ritual were forever left behind in the prescientific era. But the old myths were replaced by new myths. Ehrenwald says that myth, not to be confused with nontruth, is response to mystery; thus, the hope to eliminate myth through science was naive, and the new scientific responses to the mysteries of the universe, including the mysteries of human beings, were as much myth as the old religious responses.

However, the new script called for new actors to move to center stage. The psychotherapist replaced the cleric as healer of the soul. As Szasz notes, the "cure of [sinful] souls . . . was recast as the cure of [sick] minds" (Szasz 1978, xxiv). Furthermore, with the soul displaced by the mind and the mind regarded as a function of the brain, psychotherapy came to be regarded by many as a medical act.

The transition was now complete; the dissociation of psychotherapy from religion seemed final. Szasz points out that if the physicians of the soul could suddenly enter the contemporary world, they would be astonished to find their modern counterparts, psychotherapists, not only ignoring the assumptions that guided soul care for two millennia but also adamantly believing that psychotherapy is in no way related to earlier spiritual traditions and practices.

Contemporary Psychotherapy

Jacob Needleman observes that "modern psychiatry arose out of the vision that man must change himself and not depend for help upon an imaginary God. Over half a century ago, mainly through the insights of Freud and through the energies of those he influenced, the human psyche was wrested from the faltering hands of organized religion and was situated in the world of nature as a subject for scientific study" (Needleman 1975, 107). Such a description makes the development of modern psychotherapy seem like an unquestionable advancement. Psychotherapy has been grasped from the hands of floundering religious systems and is placed in the hands of modern science.

But is psychotherapy really all that different from the ancient soul cure procedures it replaced? Is it as scientific and distant from religion as its proponents wish to believe? Szasz does not think so. He argues that "contrition, confession, prayer, faith, inner resolution, and countless other elements are expropriated and renamed as psychotherapy; whereas certain observances, rituals, and other elements of religion are demeaned and destroyed as the symptoms of neurotic or psychotic illness" (Szasz 1978, 188). He goes on to state that "psychiatry is not merely indifferent to religion, it is implacably hostile to it. Herein lies one of the supreme ironies of modern psychotherapy: it is not merely a religion that pretends to be a science, it is actually a false religion that seeks to destroy true religion" (1978, 27–28).

Support for the assertion that psychotherapy is an alternative religious system comes from several sources. Consider, for example, the rise of the human relations movement. Thomas Oden describes encounter groups and other intensive group experiences as a demythologized, secular Judeo-Christian religion (Oden 1972). He bases this assertion on the similarities of encounter groups to Christian Pietism and Jewish Hasidism of the eighteenth and nineteenth centuries. The major similarities are intense emotional experiences (usually occurring within small groups), a zealous pursuit of honesty, a focus on "here and now" experience, interpersonal intimacy, and frequent, long, intensive meetings. A similar thesis is also developed by Paul Vitz in his book *Psychology as Religion*

(1977). Vitz argues that popular psychology, particularly what he calls "selfism," is a major American religion. Furthermore, he asserts that while this new religion has its roots in Christianity, it is deeply anti-Christian in most of its basic tenets.

According to Bregman, pop psychology is a non-traditional psychological religion that many people believe rediscovers "the essential inner core of what religion is all about, while shedding the already withered externals" (Bregman 1985, 1). Interestingly, she notes that while such an inner experience of religiousness may be viewed as a replacement for the failing religions of the West, in actuality it represents even more the failure of psychology as a science to answer religious questions (Bregman 1982, 147). Pop psychology, therefore, may be the answer to scientific psychology's failure to adequately replace religion.

Psychotherapy is not what it pretends to be. Writing in the *Journal of Operational Psychiatry* E. Mansell Pattison argues that psychotherapy is a "supernaturalistic system that parades itself as a naturalistic system" (Pattison 1977, 18). Denying its religious heritage, psychotherapy is, however, unable to escape from it. This is the Freudian dynamic of the return of the repressed: that which is denied or repressed is not eliminated; it is merely displaced from consciousness. However, as Freud pointed out, such repressed unconscious contents seldom remain unconscious. They have a way of pressing for expression and consciousness. In the case of psychotherapy, its religious roots and essential spiritual nature cannot be forever concealed. Ehrenwald notes that "it is becoming increasingly clear that the needs psychotherapy is called upon to meet transcend the naturalistic frame of reference to which it has been confined" (Ehrenwald 1966, 10). This is in large part responsible for the crisis facing contemporary psychotherapy (Pattison 1977); it is a crisis of identity.

But perhaps those most affected by this confused state of affairs are the people who seek psychotherapy for what at root may be spiritual problems. Philip Rieff describes

their plight as follows: "No longer grasping the issue between psychoanalysis and a cure of souls, many are now
entering analysis innocently, as though it were a part of
their quest for 'meaning' and 'identity'. . . . It is sad to witness their disappointment, even their bitterness; after
years of analysis, these patients have not found what they
were looking for; they have taken the wrong cure" (Rieff
1966, 92).

Christianity may very well have been faltering in its response to the needs of men and women in the late nineteenth century. In fact, Christian theology appears to
have been looking expressly to psychology for some re-
vitalization (Rieff 1966, 42). The question is whether
psychotherapy is really any better equipped to meet the
problems originally addressed by religion. Or is it even as
well equipped?

What this chapter should make clear is that psychotherapy does have a close relationship to religion. My
friend's father who thought that psychiatry had more to
do with religion than medicine appears not to have been
far wrong.

One implication of this is that it is quite appropriate to
ask how matters of spirituality relate to psychotherapy.
No longer should we be deluded into thinking that psychotherapy deals only with psychological problems and processes that are unrelated to spiritual matters. Yet is the
domain of spirituality really the same as that of psychology? If they are not identical, then in what ways are they
related? These are the questions to which we now turn.

2

Boundary Definitions and Tensions

Recognition of the religious roots of contemporary psychotherapy helps us understand some of the tension between religion and psychology or psychiatry. Many believers think that psychotherapy occupies territory stolen from its rightful owner, religion. Therefore, their suspicion of, and even antipathy toward, psychology and psychiatry is not surprising.

Determining the boundaries between psychology and religion is, therefore, a crucial matter. A clearer understanding of these boundaries should not only help to reduce the mistrust many religious people have of psychotherapists, but it should also help to resolve the identity crisis currently plaguing psychotherapy.

Boundary definition can be pursued on two levels: the practical and the theoretical. At the practical level we encounter the following sorts of questions: When should persons feeling despondent or questioning whether they are getting all they should out of life go to their pastor or priest and when should they go to a psychotherapist? When, if ever, is depression a sign of spiritual malaise and when is it a psychological problem? Or, if psychotherapy is indicated, is it important to see a Christian therapist, or can help be received from any competent therapist?

Answers to these and related questions are important and will be considered in chapter 7. However, we must first address a question of a more theoretical nature if we are to arrive at a meaningful solution to boundary tensions. This question concerns the relationship between the psychological and spiritual aspects of persons. Is the inner life of persons divisible into two parts, spiritual and psychological? If so, it is then appropriate to think of two types of problems, spiritual and psychological, with specialists in the treatment of each. In this chapter I will refer to this misconception as "psychospiritual dualism."

An alternate view is that the spiritual and psychological aspects of persons are basically identical. The assumption here is that people have only one type of nonorganic problem: it is strictly spiritual or strictly psychological. Spiritual reductionists assert that all nonorganic problems are spiritual, while psychological reductionists argue that such problems are psychological. Both agree, however, that boundary tensions are best resolved by the elimination of either psychology or religion.

Psychospiritual Dualism

Let us first examine the view of many fundamentalist and evangelical Christians on this question of the psychological and spiritual aspects of persons. Consider, for example, someone saying, "I could never feel comfortable seeing a non-Christian psychologist. How could she ever understand the spiritual side of my problem?" Or another person, questioning the validity of a standard psychological test he took as part of a job interview, who says, "But, this test doesn't address the spiritual dimension of persons. How can it ever presume to understand me when my religion is such an important part of my life?" Or finally, consider the person who argues that Christians make decisions in a fundamentally different way from non-Christians. This person claims that Christians do not rely on an intellectual analysis of the situation, nor do they merely do what they feel to be right. Rather, he believes Christians receive guidance from the Holy Spirit, whose counsel is received in their spirits.

The basic spiritual quality in people to which these individuals refer is one's relationship with God. It may not be true that this relationship is as central to personality as they think. Because Christians value this relationship so much, it is often easy for them to be mistaken about just how much difference it actually makes. However, regardless of the actual importance of a person's relationship to God, let us consider the assumption that such a relationship involves a special part of personality, the spirit.

One implication of such a view is that God does not relate to persons through the mechanisms of personality normally involved in other relationships, but through a special channel. Therefore, the ways in which we interact with other people are independent of and different from those in which we interact with God. Relationships with other people are mediated by normal psychological processes, whereas our relationship with God is mediated by the spirit and its unique processes.

If this were true, one would have cause to wonder why God created normal psychological mechanisms only to disregard them. However, the person holding such a view of spirituality might respond that God does not disregard them, but supplements them with spiritual resources. Conversion, then, means the awakening of a person's spirit, that part of a person that relates to God and through which God relates to him or her.

This dualistic view creates a radical bifurcation of personality. The psychological aspects of personality are involved in normal life and relationships. Spiritual aspects, on the other hand, have to do with only that part of personality that relates to God. Spiritual problems become problems involving one's relationship with God, and are therefore assumed to be a result of sin in the individual's life.

Case Study #3

Although George appeared to be successful and happy, several long-standing problems began to overwhelm him. One had to do with his involvement in the stock market and more recently in the high-risk arena of commodity futures. George had always dabbled in the stock market. However, over time he became more and more active in it, gradually moving from investing money he actually had, to speculating with funds he hoped to earn.

When George faced his first big loss, he suddenly had to pay his broker more money than he had or could hope to earn in the near future. He had hidden much of his financial dealings from his wife because of her concern about his involvement in the stock market. However, he told her about this loss, and together they charted a course of recovery. At his wife's insistence he went to Gamblers Anonymous, a self-help group for compulsive gamblers. However, he was not prepared to acknowledge his behavior as being compulsive or beyond his control, so after promising himself and his wife he would refrain from further stock market investments, he stopped attending the group's meetings.

Things seemed to go well for George after this incident. He worked hard, repaid his debt, and even managed to hide his family's financial struggles from everyone else. Then suddenly his world collapsed. A routine tax audit of his business turned up the fact that to repay his debt he had borrowed much of the money from his business but had done so in a way that was of questionable legality. George was threatened with a large tax penalty and a possible charge of fraud.

George responded to this crisis with overwhelming panic and depression. He had always been somewhat prone to depression, particularly in times of stress, but this time he hit bottom so hard that his doctor was worried about a possible suicide attempt. He immediately started

George on medication and told him it might be necessary to consider a psychiatric hospitalization if the depression did not break within a few days.

George's pastor came to visit him at this point, having heard of his troubles from George's wife. He supported the doctor's prescription of medication and a psychiatric hospitalization should that become necessary. However, after listening to George's account of his troubles, he expressed the opinion that the medical interventions were superficial responses to a much deeper problem, a problem that he judged to be spiritual. He felt that George had broken God's law and that his depression and associated problems were consequences of this violation. He did not say that God was somehow directly punishing George for his sin, but suggested that George's failure to obey God's standards had certain natural consequences.

The pastor believed that George could resolve his problems only by confessing his sins and changing his behavior. Calling his problem a spiritual problem was to say that it was essentially a disruption of George's relationship with God caused by breaking God's law. Specifically, the pastor felt that George's core problem was greed and materialism. His risk taking and the questionable business arrangements precipitating his current crisis were byproducts of his idolatrous love of money. A secondary but related cause of his problems, according to the pastor, was George's duplicity. The attempt to hide his financial dealings from his wife was a breach of God's pattern for marriage, and this act of deception he then followed with devious or dishonest business arrangements. Both of these underlying causes of his problems were sins, and that rendered the crisis a spiritual one.

If such an assessment of the causes and dynamics of George's problems is correct, are the problems really of a different sort from those we might call purely psychological? Does a person experience them differently from psychological problems, and do they involve different parts of the personality? To examine these questions, let us consider something that perhaps could be viewed as a more typical psychological problem.

Case Study #4

Most of her friends did not think that Elizabeth had a problem, but that was simply because many of them had the same problem. Elizabeth was overweight. In spite of her doctor's urgings and in spite of her repeated efforts at diets and various weight-loss programs, she remained approximately sixty pounds overweight and hopelessly out of control of her eating.

It was her admission of the latter that finally led Elizabeth to set an appointment at an eating disorders clinic at a local hospital. Here she was seen by a psychologist who, after a battery of tests and an assessment interview, diagnosed her problem as compulsive overeating. Elizabeth confessed with some embarrassment that she would periodically binge on large amounts of junk food, preventing further weight gain by following this with several days of fasting. Her life was dominated by food, for she spent much of her time planning when and what she would eat.

The psychological tests showed that Elizabeth was quite depressed. In fact, she had probably been depressed for years. Although it was not a massive depression of the sort that would incapacitate her, it was still clinically significant. It at least went back to the death of her husband seven years before, although its roots were even deeper as Elizabeth reported having had serious episodes of depression even in adolescence. It was at this stage of her life that she developed eating as a strategy for soothing her hurt and sad feelings. Years of practice had thus resulted in a full-blown eating disorder. The psychologist's analysis of Elizabeth's problems was that the causes of her compulsive overeating were an underlying depression and an unconscious strategy to eliminate this depression through the abuse of food. But George's problems also involved depression and compulsive behavior. How do these prob-

lems differ or on what basis is one considered spiritual
and the other psychological?

Differential Diagnosis of Spiritual
and Psychological Problems

As practiced by advocates of psychospiritual dualism,
differentiation of psychological and spiritual problems de-
mands first ruling out spiritual problems. Thus, if a problem is not the result of personal sin it is judged to be
psychological in nature. This does not mean that the person is free from sin, but that sin does not seem to be at the
root of the specific problem under investigation. Thus, in
the case of Elizabeth, her depression and compulsive use
of food to cope with feelings are neither sinful in themselves nor a result of or response to some more basic,
underlying sin. Her problem is, therefore, considered to be
psychological.

This sort of thinking is common to many evangelical
Christians. It is the position also taken by many Christian
counselors or therapists. Some might disagree with our
specific analyses of the two case studies; however, they
would agree that problems can be viewed profitably as
either spiritual or psychological. They may also disagree
as to what constitutes one or the other type of problem.
All psychospiritual dualists, however, seem to hold to a
differentiation of spiritual and psychological diagnoses
and treatments. Let us briefly consider several representatives of such a view.

Dr. Frank Minirth, psychiatrist and adjunct professor of
practical theology at Dallas Theological Seminary, states
in his book *Christian Psychiatry* (1970) that the first task of
the Christian counselor attempting to help someone is differential diagnosis. Minirth bases the necessity for this on
the fact that humans consist of three parts—body, soul,
and spirit. He defines the soul as the psychological part of
personality. It consists of the mind, emotions, and the will.
In contrast, "the spirit is the supernatural part of man giv-

en at birth" (1970, 66). It is "the organ for communion with God" (1970, 66). Finally, the body is the physical part of a person.

These distinctions are not novel to Minirth, nor does he claim as much. Rather, they are part of a long-standing tradition in theology, a tradition generally referred to as the trichotomistic view of persons. More interesting here, however, than Minirth's theology is the psychology that grows out of such a position. The soul and spirit are viewed as being independent; the Spirit of God provides the human spirit with a perception that "comes from deep within and is independent of mental reasoning" (1970, 66). Minirth underscores this independence of spiritual perception from the normal processes of psychological reasoning by enumerating ways to determine whether a particular impression is from the spirit or from the soul. While he goes on to discuss some ways in which spirit and soul interact, he clearly shows them to be separate, arguing that the spirit is the innermost part of a person while soul and body are the more exterior aspects of personhood.

Based on these distinctions, Minirth says that the psychotherapist must evaluate persons at the spiritual, psychological, and physical levels. He proposes that spiritual problems can be classified as one of four basic types: the need for salvation, the need to grow in Christian maturity, the need to deal with some specific sin, and demonic problems. He also catalogues types of psychological problems and physical problems and suggests treatments for each.

Another popular Christian author whose writings reflect psychospiritual dualism is the Swiss physician Dr. Paul Tournier. Although his position is more complex than Minirth's, it is guided by the same assumption— spiritual and psychological aspects of personhood should be distinguished.

This is made clear in his book *The Strong and the Weak*. Discussing the differences between true or objective guilt

and guilty feelings, Tournier says that true guilt follows a
breach of God's divine law. In contrast, guilty feelings are
frequently due to a false or neurotic guilt that is subjec-
tively experienced in the same way, but in which no such
sin is involved. Based on this, Tournier suggests the need
to distinguish "two orders of phenomena: the natural and
the supernatural, those that constitute our physiological
and psychological reactions and those which arise from
our spiritual life, from the action of God in us" (Tournier
1963, 213). He says that to fail to recognize the differences
between psychological and spiritual problems is to run
the risk of treating a person for the wrong problem.

Tournier does not, however, separate these two spheres
as radically as Minirth. After emphasizing the dangers of
failure to engage in differential diagnosis, he goes on to
warn that "it is no less dangerous, however, to under-
estimate the constant mutual influence of the two orders
of phenomena" (1963, 214). He argues that such an under-
estimation is to completely misunderstand the nature of
persons; it is to "miss the meaning of incarnation and to
forget that our supernatural destiny is constantly involved
in our natural life" (1963, 214). He goes on to say that we
cannot draw a neat dividing line between spiritual and
psychological spheres. We can only look to God for guidance and through self-examination come to discern in ourselves the distinction.

Evaluation

The advocates of psychospiritual dualism concede that
the differential diagnosis of psychological and spiritual
problems is difficult. But is it necessary, or even possible?
And is it a meaningful way to regard a person?

One consequence of separating the spiritual from the
psychological aspects of persons is a trivialization of the
spiritual dimension of personhood. When "spirit" is identified as "that part of us that relates to God," suddenly we
are in the position of relating to God with only part of our

total beings. It is then only a short step to believing that God is more interested in certain aspects of us than in others. The dividing line between the sacred and the secular then cuts right through the fabric of personality. In the resulting fragmentation a person becomes a collection of assorted parts, some of more value than others.

A particularly clear example of this tendency is found in *Emotional Problems and the Gospel,* where Vernon Grounds struggles with the difficult realization that Christians are often characterized as having poor mental health. After a review of the data relevant to this issue he states: "Far from serving as a panacea for psychic difficulties, religion, even our own unique faith, often proves of little, no, or minus value with respect to healthy mindedness" (Grounds 1966, 107–8). However, his response to this situation is even more disturbing than the original phenomenon. He goes on to say that "fundamentally and finally, Christianity is not concerned with the individual's emotional welfare any more than it is concerned with his physical condition. Fundamentally and finally, Christianity is concerned about the individual's relationship to God" (1966, 11).

This view of persons seems incompatible with Scripture where sanctification, or spiritual growth after conversion, is presented as the process of becoming whole. Sanctification is the restoration of the entirety of our beings, reversing the effects of sin and making us mature or complete in Christ (Col. 1:28). There is no notion here of God working in only one part of us. Salvation was designed to restore the total personality, for God is interested in every part of us.

Another consequence of attempting to separate spiritual and psychological aspects of persons is that spirituality then often comes to be equated with morality. Spiritual problems are associated with sin and spiritual health with holiness. While there is no doubt that these are the fundamental dynamics of spiritual life, is spirituality really nothing more than personal holiness? Is not something lost when the rich inner life of communion with God gets reduced to morality and personal piety?

Wolfhart Pannenberg (1983) argues that such a constricted view of spirituality is an unfortunate consequence of connecting guilt consciousness with piety. He believes that guilt consciousness is not an inherent part of Christian spirituality; however, it has often been assumed to be so because the Christian message is so intimately connected with forgiveness of sins and redemption from the power of sin. Protestantism, which has often emphasized awareness of personal sinfulness as a condition of faith, has run the risk of keeping people in a state of bondage to sin through the very consciousness of sin that was intended to produce freedom. Pannenberg argues that this has also led to a diminished spirituality wherein the egocentric preoccupation with one's sinfulness blocks a fuller awareness of and response to God.

Another weakness of psychospiritual dualism is that it limits the psychological aspects of persons to whatever is left over after we take out those parts of people that relate to God. These psychological aspects become secondary mechanisms in human personality, for the "real stuff" of personality is deemed to be spiritual. The psychological sphere is somehow supposed to be different from and independent of the real or deepest self, the spiritual self.

The effort of psychospiritual dualists to distinguish the spiritual from the psychological may be helpful if spirituality is not removed too far from the realm of psychological functions. Tournier's writings represent such a moderate position. By calling attention to the spiritual aspects of human experience and by emphasizing the mutual interaction of the spiritual and psychological spheres, he guards against a psychology that has no place for spirituality.

However, to remove the spiritual from the psychological realm is to render the psychological aspects of persons irrelevant to spirituality, which in turn leads to some highly implausible conclusions. One, for example, is that we do not relate to God with our minds or emotions, in that these are psychological mechanisms. And yet Christian literature, and Scripture itself, make clear that we do relate to God with minds and with emotions. And if this is so, then the psychological mechanisms that mediate our relationship with God are the same as those that are involved in relationships with anyone else. Therefore, we believe that psychological and spiritual aspects of persons are not as distinct from each other as the psychospiritual dualists want to make them.

Spiritual Reductionism

For some people, differential diagnosis of spiritual and psychological problems is unnecessary, because they contend that all problems lacking a physiological basis are spiritual. In their view psychology is an illegitimate discipline in that it moves into the domain of religion, and with the pseudoauthority of science claims that "religious" problems are psychological ones. It then sets itself up as having the unique expertise with which to treat these problems.

In their book *The Psychological Way/The Spiritual Way* Martin and Diedre Bobgan state the following: "From its very beginning psychotherapy was developed as an alternate means of healing, *not* as an addition or complement to Christianity or any other religion. Psychotherapy is not only offered as an alternate or substitute method of healing troubled souls, but also as a surrogate religion" (Bobgan and Bobgan 1979, 182). The Bobgans assert, however, that nonmedical problems reside not in the mind but in the spirit. Psychotherapy addresses the mind and therefore misses the real problem—a spiritual problem residing in the deepest core of personality, the spirit.

According to the Bobgans not only does psychotherapy

miss the mark and fail to treat the real problem, it also serves to strengthen a part of personality that should be weakened. Psychotherapy treats the "old nature," which we are instructed in Scripture to crucify. Quite in contrast to crucifying these aspects of self, psychotherapy builds them up. Mind (or soul) and spirit are thus in opposition to each other; to strengthen the one is to weaken the other. Thus viewed, psychotherapy is an enemy of the spirit in that it is directed toward the strengthening of the soul. It does this through the treatment of the mind, will, and emotions, which are functions of the soul.

Another representative of the spiritual reductionist position, Charles Solomon, makes a similar point. He argues as follows: "Psychotherapy then has as its goal to help a person become stronger and stronger. But God says we must become weaker and weaker that He might become our strength. . . . Thus psychotherapy is at cross purposes with God and becomes a substitute for the work of the Holy Spirit" (Solomon 1971, 27).

These charges that psychotherapy is fundamentally in opposition to Christianity are serious ones. We should note, however, that while psychotherapy may strengthen aspects of self that should be crucified, this is not an essential part of the psychotherapeutic process. At its best psychotherapy can be a powerful resource in spiritual growth. It helps persons to identify and crucify their false selves and thereby see themselves as they are: spiritual beings destined to be in loving and submissive relationship with God.

However, according to spiritual reductionists psychotherapy is not the appropriate route to solving our problems or finding help for our inner dis-ease. Arguing that "the Bible is the repository of the healing balm for all non-organically based mental-emotional disorders," the Bobgans assert that the cure for people experiencing disturbances in emotions, behavior, or thought is found in trusting and following the spiritual principles of the Bible (1977, 11). Spiritual counseling thus should lead a person to such a response. It is the only means of addressing the real root of so-called psychological problems.

Jay Adams is another popular proponent of this position. In his book *Competent to Counsel* he states:

> Scriptures plainly speak of both organically based problems as well as those problems that stem from sinful attitudes and behavior; but where, in all of God's Word, is there so much as a trace of any third source of problems which might approximate the modern concept of "mental illness"? Clearly the burden of proof lies with those who loudly affirm the existence of mental illness or disease but fail to demonstrate biblically that it exists. Until such a demonstration is forthcoming, the only safe course to follow is to declare with all of Scripture that the genesis of such human problems is twofold, not threefold. (Adams 1970, 29)

Adams, therefore, roots all nonorganic problems in personal sin. Such problems are spiritual and the only appropriate treatment of them is to expose the underlying sinful attitude or behavior and encourage confession and repentance.

Evaluation

This and the next position we shall consider are difficult to critique in that there is an elegance to them that comes from their parsimony. Here we have none of the confusion of psychological and spiritual processes that we found in the dualist position. Psychological processes are relabeled as spiritual and there is only one sphere of interiority, the spiritual.

If spirituality were understood in broader terms, this position might be more tenable. But these authors reduce it to morality and posit personal sin behind every nonorganic problem. (Carl Jung spoke of all problems after age thirty-five as being spiritual, but by the term *spiritual* he meant something much broader than personal sin.)

Thus, the major problem with spiritual reductionism is less the assertion that all problems are spiritual than the meaning these authors assign to spirituality.

The tendency of spiritual reductionists to base all problems in personal sin is also incompatible with Scripture. In addressing the disciples' question about sin as the cause of a man's blindness, Jesus said that no one's sin was responsible for his blindness. The man was born blind so that God could be glorified by Jesus' healing of him (John 9:1–5). This answer by Jesus suggests that it is equally erroneous to identify personal sin as the cause of all psychological problems.

Sin in an ultimate sense may very well be behind all problems, inasmuch as one result of the fall is that we live in a sinful world. But not only do we sin; we also are sinned against. If we consider the effects of the sinful ways in which others treat us as well as of the ways in which we ourselves sin, we may then say sin lies behind all psychological problems. If, however, we only blame the sins the troubled person commits, the assertion that sin lies behind every problem is dangerously wrong. The danger lies in the damage that is easily and often unavoidably done to the suffering person. The original problems are compounded with neurotic guilt, and the person is left worse off than before.

An additional problem associated with the spiritual reductionist position is that, while it emphasizes sin, it tends to hold a naive and shallow understanding of it. To associate sin with one part of personality exclusively (i.e., the soul or the mind) is to fail to appreciate the doctrine of total depravity. Every aspect of a person is polluted with sin. The seat of sin cannot, therefore, be located in the mind or the emotions as the Bobgans wish it to be. Psychotherapy is not necessarily the enemy of Christian spirituality just because it addresses a person's emotions and mind.

Richard Lovelace believes that the weakness of Adams's form of spiritual reductionism is that it regards sin as merely "habit patterns of disobedience which can be broken down by the application of will power working in a process of dehabituation" (Lovelace 1979, 220). Lovelace notes that such treatment may help in situations where a person has been looking for easy victories of faith and ignoring the necessary vigorous engagement of the will. However, he says that it will usually deal only with the surface manifestations of sin, leaving untouched the deeper roots that are not adequately understood or addressed by such counseling. The result of this can be a pharisaical self-righteousness in which persons may actually be worse off after the so-called help than before, the delusion of righteousness removing them further from the truth and usually making it less accessible to them.

Psychological Reductionism

Even more common than spiritual reductionism is the position that all problems are basically psychological or even physical. Psychological reductionism maintains that religion has provided a prescientific perspective on persons that is more fully and accurately presented in modern psychology. Here religious explanations of the causes of problems are considered to be at best naive and at worst misguided and dangerous. However, psychological reductionism assumes the same stances as spiritual reductionism: There is only one kind of problem and one internal process.

Reductionism has always been one of psychology's greatest points of offense to Christians. And with no surprise. Consider the following statement of J. B. Watson:

> Human beings do not want to class themselves with other animals. They are willing to admit that they are animals but "something else, in addition." It is this "something else" that causes the trouble. In this "something else" is bound up everything that is classed as religion, the life hereafter, morals. . . . The raw fact is that you, as a psychologist, if you are to remain scientific, must describe the be-

havior of man in no other terms than those you would use
in describing the behavior of an ox. (Watson 1930, v)

At the other end of the psychological spectrum, Freud
also illustrates how simple it is to reduce spiritual and religious phenomena to psychological processes. Freud
explained mysticism as a regressive reactivation of the
infant's lack of ego boundaries (1930, 65–72), and later
as "the obscure self-perception of the realm outside the
ego, of the id" (1938, 300). Freud viewed religion not only
reductionistically but also with a strong psychopathologi-
cal bias. Over the course of his writings he compared religion to a psychosis (paranoia), a neurosis (obsessive-
compulsive disorder), and an infantile neurosis. He also
dubbed it a manifestation of the Oedipus complex, a mass
delusion, a neurotic relic, and "blissful hallucinatory confusion." He explained spirits and demons as "projections
of man's own emotional impulses" (1913, 92), and God as
the displacement of oedipal ambivalence and as a cosmic
projection of the father complex (1910, 123). Anyone familiar with his work realizes that Freud was preoccupied with
religion all his life and found himself returning to it continuously in his writings.

Eric Fromm is another good representative of psychological reductionism. His position is more subtle than that
of Freud or Watson, and he is clearly less reductionistic than either one of them. He argues, however, that
psychology is better able to explain and solve the problems and phenomena encountered by religion. In *Psychoanalysis and Religion* Fromm discusses the common
ground between religion and psychoanalysis.

> I want to show in these pages that it not true that we have
> to give up the concern for the soul if we do not accept the
> tenets of religion. The psychoanalyst is in a position to
> study the human reality behind religion as well as behind
> nonreligious symbol systems. He finds that the question is
> not whether man returns to religion and believes in God
> but whether he lives love and thinks truth. If he does so the

symbol systems he uses are of secondary importance. If he does not they are of no importance. (Fromm 1950, 9)

Both religion and psychoanalysis are concerned with helping people live more fully. Religion is useful to the degree it does this. What it does beyond this is superfluous.

Fromm goes on to further describe this common core, first identifying what he perceives to be shared by all great world religions.

Man must strive to recognize the truth and can be fully human only to the extent to which he succeeds in this task. He must be independent and free, an end in himself and not the means for any other person's purposes. He must relate himself to his fellow man lovingly. If he has no love, he is an empty shell even if his were all power, wealth, and intelligence. Man must know the difference between good and evil, he must learn to listen to the voice of his conscience and be able to follow it. . . . The aim of the psychoanalytic cure of the soul is to help the patient attain the attitude which I just described as religious. (1950, 73–74)

Fromm thus views religion with tolerance but also with condescension: psychotherapy accomplishes the same ends as religion, but it does so without the trappings of dogma or religious symbols.

Evaluation

British neuropsychologist Donald MacKay claims that explanations do not have to be reductionistic (MacKay 1974). It is quite possible to describe persons from a number of different vantage points, none of which precludes the truth or usefulness of the other. Reductionistic explanations, on the other hand, assert that only one vantage point (or level of explanation) represents truth and that all others are unnecessary at best and illusory at worst.

MacKay illustrates this notion of various levels of analysis by using the analogy of an electronic sign (1974, 37–38).

A scientist giving an explanation of the sign might exhaustively describe its workings in terms of the physics and chemistry of its electrical activity and yet completely exclude any reference to the sign's message, that is, to its significance. The scientist's explanation is reductionistic in that it attempts to analyze the sign at the simplest possible level. However, it only becomes an offensive act of reductionism should the scientist assert that this is all there is to the sign and that its message or meaning is negated by the physiochemical explanation.

In his attempt to reconcile behavioral psychology with Christian theology, Rodger Bufford adopts this levels-of-analysis approach to argue for what he calls "modified reductionism" (Bufford 1981, 39–40). He suggests that the simplest or most basic explanation does not make all higher levels of analysis and their respective explanations redundant, but that they complement each other. Thus, the basic level of analysis of any phenomenon is to place it within the framework of the laws of physics. However, in order to truly understand the phenomenon, higher levels of analysis will also be necessary. In fact, Bufford suggests that in terms of ultimate meaning, the most abstract or general level of analysis is actually the most significant.

Edwin Wallace argues somewhat similarly with regard to Freudian reductionism. If psychoanalysis tends to be too reductionistic in its approach to religion, theology tends to be too antireductionistic, jumping too quickly to the highest level of explanation (Wallace 1983, 53). From this Wallace concludes that each of the different levels of explanation is incomplete in itself, but that they complement each other.

Wallace does, however, criticize Freud's works on religion on a number of grounds. He points out that Freud's "psychopathologizing" of religion reflects his personal judgments, which were not conflict free. These judgments were not based on the results of Freud's psychoanalytic work with religious patients as much as they were a speculative extrapolation of his own ideas, prejudices, and religious conflicts. Moreover, Wallace observes that while Freud may have been correct in noting some similarities between religion and neurosis, he failed to correctly understand the significance of this similarity.

While Freudian explanations of religion may contribute to our understanding of the psychological processes undergirding the religious experience, there is no basis for arguing that they explain away that experience or are themselves the essence of religion. For fleeting moments, Freud himself seemed aware of this. For example, he stated that merely because something is an illusion (derived from human wishes) does not mean it is necessarily false (1927, 31). And as early as 1913 he asserted that his theories did not exhaust the explanation of religious phenomena, but merely added a new facet to them (1913, 157). Thus, while mysticism may indeed involve a regressive reactivation of infantile ego boundaries, this is certainly not the last word on the phenomenon. A Freudian explanation of mysticism assists us in understanding the psychological substrata of the experience; it certainly does not explain the experience away or tell us anything about its essence, meaning, or value.

Although Fromm's tolerance of religion may be preferable to the intolerance of Watson, Freud, or other more radical reductionists, the danger of Fromm's position should not be underestimated. If psychology replaces religion but does not deal with human spiritual longings or the means for their fulfillment, it replaces it not with some advanced truth but with a lie.

Toward a Broadened View of Spirituality

In his discussion of the relationship between psychology and spirituality, Robert Doran notes two extreme positions that must be avoided. The first is the reduction of spirituality to psychology, wherein spiritual experience is "nothing but" some psychological mechanism. This

extreme position is represented by psychological reductionism. The second equally fatal error is to divorce
spirituality from psychology so completely that "spirituality becomes a separate realm of human activity that is
not integrated with psychological reality" (Doran 1979,
858). This, we concluded, is the problem with the dualist
position. It is also the problem with the spiritual reductionist position inasmuch as it is so extremely limited as to
render the spiritual and psychological spheres of personality unrelated.

What we need, therefore, is a broadened view of spirituality and a way of intimately relating it to and placing it
within the overall framework of psychospiritual functions
and processes of personality. Lovelace supports the logic
of this necessity when he writes that we cannot isolate
spiritual and psychological problems by treating the latter nonspiritually or the former nonpsychologically, "because the human soul is a psychospiritual continuum in
which psychological stress, physical conditions and spiritual states are deeply interrelated" (Lovelace 1979, 220).

In pursuit of such a psychospiritual continuum, chapter 3 will address the psychological understanding of
spirituality. In chapter 4 we will address the issue by reviewing Christian spirituality. In chapter 5, we will develop a model of psychospirituality that avoids the pitfalls
we have just observed, and that establishes and supports
the deep interdependence of the psychological and spiritual aspects of persons.

3

Psychology and Spirituality

Although many psychologists have viewed spirituality in a reductionistic manner, there are a number of significant exceptions. In this chapter we will review four systems of psychology that accommodate spirituality: analytical psychology, We-psychology, existential psychology, and contemplative psychology.

This is not a comprehensive survey of all the psychologies that address spirituality. Robert Assagioli's psychosynthesis, Victor Frankl's logotherapy, and a number of lesser known approaches identified with transpersonal psychology share an interest in spirituality. The sample we will consider has been selected for consideration because these approaches seem to hold particular promise to enrich and assist our understanding of Christian spirituality. With the exception of Jung, who saw his work as providing an alternate conceptualization of spirituality to Christianity's, the theorists treated in this chapter saw themselves as working within historic Christianity and viewed their insights as being compatible with Christian truth.

Analytical Psychology: Carl Jung

Probably no theorist in psychology is more closely con-

nected with spirituality than Carl Jung (1875–1961). Even
as Freud was "against" religion Jung was "for" it. Szasz
points out that the fundamental difference between Freud
and Jung was the basic attitude with which they ap-
proached the phenomena they studied. Jung regarded
both religion and neuroses with respect, viewing religion
as collective mythologies and neuroses as individual ones.
On the other hand, Freud regarded both religion and neuroses contemptuously, religion as a neurosis and neuroses
as defenses against reality. Thus, Szasz argues, in Jungian
psychology religion came to be seen as an indispensable
spiritual support, while in Freudian psychology it was
seen as an illusory crutch (Szasz 1978, 173).

Jung's tolerance of religion must surely have been due
in part to his religious background. Eight of his uncles
were clergymen, and his father was a Lutheran pastor.
However, his father struggled all his life with the validity
of his faith, and early on, Jung concluded that his father's
misery was due to the failure of the Christian myth. The
theme of his autobiography *Memories Dreams Reflections*
(Jung 1961) is the search for an alternate myth, a myth that
would save himself and others from the fate of his father,
whom he viewed with pity. Commenting on this, Philip
Rieff points out that Jung began with the premise of the
failure of Christianity and other Western religions, and
that he spent his life looking for a "functional equivalent
in psychotherapy to what he assumed must have been the
therapeutic effect of Christian imagery and institutions"
(Rieff 1966, 109).

Rieff argues that, although Jung is overtly more sympathetic to religion than Freud, when his work is examined
from either a Christian or Jewish perspective, it is actually
more heretical. He suggests that by making religiosity in-
stinctual Jung makes it too natural, "so natural, in fact,
that it can scarcely serve the purpose of any particular historic faith" (1966, 91). He goes on to argue that "Jung developed a fresh rhetoric of spirituality, without the bother
of churches or the imposition of consequential ethics"

(1966, 114)—"a private religiosity without institutional reference or communal membership" (1966, 134). No longer the transcendent God of the historic Judeo-Christian faith, Jung's God is interior. He is the subterranean God who inhabits the collective unconscious.

Christians have had a hard time determining whether Jung is friend or foe. Sanford (1968) and Kelsey (1968) are two well-known authors who have promoted Jung's psychological insights as important aids to Christian growth. Similarly, the sizable percentage of Jungian analysts who are theologically trained attests to the appeal of his system to the religious. Still others have argued that Jung's guidelines for soul cure are of a completely different order than those of spiritual transformation in Christ (Buber 1952; Hillman 1972).

Jung himself showed some interest in the relationship between his system of thought and Christianity. In "Psychoanalysis and the Cure of Souls" Jung argued that both analysis and pastoral care are concerned with the cure of souls. However, he went on to distinguish between them by suggesting that while analysis cures souls by reinforcing the natural drive toward wholeness that exists within a person, pastoral care supplies answers and meaning that are outside the individual (Jung 1936).

It is not possible here to provide a comprehensive presentation or evaluation of Jung's system of psychology. His theory is too complex and, as already noted, its relationship to Christianity is quite unclear. Our more modest objective will be to first examine his view of spirituality and then attempt to evaluate its usefulness.

The central concept in Jung's view of spiritual growth is that of *individuation*—the lifelong process of becoming whole through the synthesis of conscious and unconscious aspects of personality. In more technical terms, Jung defined it as the establishment of a relationship between the ego (which is the center of consciousness) and the self (which is the innermost center, extending beyond consciousness to include the unconscious). Jung considered individuation to be a religious process, describing it as the submission of the ego-will to God's will (Jung 1975, 265). Jung thus viewed spiritual growth as the movement away from the ego as the center of personality toward the self as that center.

The self in Jungian psychology is a somewhat mystical concept. Verda Heisler, in an article entitled "The Transpersonal in Jungian Theory and Therapy," suggests that the Jungian self "extends from the psyche of the individual into the far reaches of the universe as a container of the divine creative force which is unfolded in the development of man but which also far transcends not only the human individual but also the human race" (Heisler 1973, 337–38). The self, according to Jung, is the true center of personality; the ego should only be a way station toward integration. The problem is that people tend to get stuck in ego-centeredness. However, the wholeness that is the goal of the spiritual quest cannot be obtained apart from movement to the self as center.

More concretely, what this entails is the process of integrating the various complementary and conflicting elements of personality into the self. Of particular importance in this process is the integration of the "shadow." The shadow consists of those psychic qualities which, because of their incompatibility with conscious values and goals, have been denied a place in the person's consciousness. These suppressed aspects of personality must be integrated with the rest of personality if we are to become the authentic and whole persons that we should be.

Integration, therefore, is transcendence beyond the limited, selective, and even deceptive functioning of ego-centeredness. We attain this road to salvation through increased consciousness, that is, through increasing our knowledge of ourselves. Jung felt that when we become aware of the opposites inherent in human nature, and in our own natures in particular, we then not only know ourselves but we also know God. According to Jung, "the God image does not coincide with the unconscious as such but with a special component of it, namely, the archetype of the self" (Jung 1977, 469). Spiritual growth is thus the discovery of this God image and the integration of it into the rest of the personality.

Jung's contributions to the psychology of spirituality are many. His psychology of religious experience allowed him to remove religion from the realm of neuroses and place it firmly within the realm of creative expressions of the deepest aspects of the self. In so doing he restored the religious function to psychic life. Furthermore, his discovery of the important role of symbols in the integration of the psyche is a major contribution to our understanding of the place of symbol and liturgy in religious life. Spirituality and psychology are deeply interconnected.

Jung's teaching that both spiritual and psychological health depend upon an open relationship between conscious and unconscious forces in personality is a significant step in strengthening the concept of spirituality. Perhaps more than any other depth psychologist Jung has shown the way toward integrating the conscious and unconscious aspects of personality. Furthermore, his recognition of the importance of the individual's ability to transcend incomplete conceptions of the self as a step in spiritual growth is helpful. His discussion of psychological types is valuable for understanding the unique ways in which different individuals experience and express their relationship with God. And finally, his criterion for the discernment of true and false spirituality is a most valuable contribution to a psychology of spirituality. It was his suggestion that the integration of a person's inner and outer worlds is the major way in which true and false spirituality, as well as mysticism and psychosis, may be distinguished from each other. Such a distinction has important implications for spiritual development.

However, when evaluated in the light of historic Christianity, the major limitation of Jung's view of spirituality is its failure to adequately represent God's transcendence or to provide for our self-transcendence. In Rieff's words,

"Jung's is a religious doctrine in which God is rendered completely interior. The 'Thou' term becomes a function of the 'I' " (Rieff 1966, 97). In this process, self is deified and God is psychologized.

Jung's interiorized God is a totally immanent God; the God of Christianity is immanent and yet transcendent. His salvation, therefore, allows for our transcendence beyond and above ourselves. In fact, as we shall see later, Christian spirituality has always viewed such self-transcendence as essential to spiritual growth. While Jung builds self-transcendence into his model, in actuality he remains much closer to self-fulfillment (Kopas 1981, 220).

In his analysis of the relationship between Jungian psychology and Christian spirituality, Robert Doran concludes that Jung's contribution to Christian spirituality may be more to "help us recognize inordinate projections and disoriented affections than in orienting us positively to the God of the Christian faith and to Christ" (Doran 1979, 858). The reason for this fatal limitation is, according to Doran, that "the innermost region of our interiority is . . . no longer ourselves, but the place of grace, where the gift of God's love is poured forth into our hearts by the Holy Spirit who has been given to us" (1979, 861). Jung interprets this innermost center not in terms of grace but of nature. Doran argues that this equation of God and self makes prayer talking to oneself, thus destroying the self's transcendent experience of genuine Christian spirituality.

Instead of providing an understanding of genuine Christian spirituality, Jung has developed an alternative to it, a kind of psychological spirituality. This is an ever present danger in psychology. The prominent Jungian theorist Jolande Jacobi seems to support such an interpretation:

> Jungian psychology is . . . a way of healing and a way of salvation. It has the power to cure. . . . In addition it knows the way and has the means to lead the individual to his "salvation," to the knowledge and fulfillment of his personality, which have always been the aim of spiritual strivings. . . .

> Apart from its medical aspect, Jungian psychotherapy is
> thus a system of education and spiritual guidance. (Jacobi
> 1973, 60)

It may be helpful to distinguish Jung's significant contributions to spirituality in general from his more limited
contributions to the understanding of distinctively Christian spirituality. His focus is basically on natural spirituality, that is, the native soil out of which either genuine
Christian spirituality or some alternate spirituality de-
velops. (This distinction will be further developed in chapter 5.) Such a distinction allows us to take many of Jung's
insights and apply them to Christian spirituality without
having to assume that his model of spirituality is either en-
tirely correct or totally adequate. Jung demonstrates the
ways in which spirituality is rooted in personality and
thereby provides a preliminary map of the relationship between spirituality and psychology.

While a personality centered in self is undoubtedly
healthier and closer to wholeness than one centered in
ego, it still falls far short of Christian salvation. In Christian salvation the self is grounded and centered in Jesus
Christ and is, thereby, renewed into the image in which it
was originally created. We then have more than integration of personality; what we have is the indwelling of a new
spirit within us, the Holy Spirit, and the outworking of his
life within ours. Jungian psychology, therefore, provides a
valuable picture of natural spirituality. It is, however, a
poor substitute for genuine Christian spirituality.

We-Psychology: Fritz Kunkel

Fritz Kunkel (1889-1956) built on Jung's work while
managing to avoid the major limitations of the Jungian
vision of spirituality. Kunkel was a disciple and colleague
of Alfred Adler and corresponded with Jung. He sought to
develop an explicitly religious psychology based on a syn-

thesis of Freud, Adler, and Jung. His starting point was the question of why it is so difficult to move beyond ego-centricity. Jung emphasized knowledge as the vehicle for movement beyond egocentricity, but Kunkel thought that more was necessary. His objective was to understand the development and operation of egocentricity, which he believed to be the major obstacle to surrendering to God.

Kunkel roots egocentricity in early childhood, viewing it to be a natural adjustment to the child's egocentric environment. He describes it as "a normal reaction to an abnormal situation . . . the absence of the right kind of love" (Sanford 1984, 54–55). Because parental love is always egocentric to some degree, it is therefore incomplete. As a result, the child always sustains narcissistic injuries of one sort or another, and the child's defense against these is egocentricity. This is a revolt against the earlier, innate "original we-feeling" which, according to Kunkel, is the capacity of the young child to integrate experience with others as a part of the self. In fact, Kunkel notes that the self is not synonymous with one's own self; rather, it always includes the "we-experience," the experience of interpersonal connectedness. A return to the we-feelings of the pre-egocentric child is, in Kunkel's view, our hope for growth and wholeness. In contrast to other approaches to psychology, Kunkel argues for this ego-transcendent self as the route to we-experiences with others and with God.

While this broader view of self may have been implicit in Jung, he de-emphasized the importance of others in both the emergence of the self and its continuing functioning. However, others are indispensable for self in Kunkel's thought. In fact, the sterility of egocentric life is precisely due to our being cut off from the creativity and energy that come from our relationships with others at our deepest center. Relationships with others may, in fact, be present for the egocentric person. However, until egocentricity is rooted out of the very core of our personality, we will not experience the deep connectedness with others that Kunkel calls "the we-experience."

The breach of the infant's original connection with the mother and others (the breach of the original we) leads to egocentricity. In essence this involves the substitution of a sham center, the ego, for the real center, the self. But because the ego (me) is much more constricted than the self (me-in-relationships), the result is alienation. The ego subsequently becomes more and more brittle as it is called upon to do a job which it was never intended or equipped to do. The ego thus becomes a protective shell around the personality. However, this leaves a person stripped of the resources needed to live, and ultimately egocentricity leads to a crisis. Kunkel views this crisis as the only hope for movement beyond egocentricity.

> In any form the crisis simply leads to the realization growing out of uncomfortable experiences that there is a need for a readjustment of one's thinking and behavior. The individual comes to feel that he must do something different. Old ways of behaving are no longer satisfactory, so new ones must be adopted. A turning point has been reached. There may be a total collapse of the whole Ego-pattern or merely a minor modification of some one of its elements. (Sanford 1984, 140)

Kunkel continues, "The egocentric form of psychic life breaks down because it proves to be erroneous in its content and too rigid in its form. The attempts of the individual to save his Ego only lead him nearer to the crisis" (Sanford 1984, 149).

Kunkel suggests that this is the meaning of Christ's paradoxical teaching that he who would save his life must lose it. In order to save our lives, that is, to really live, we must lose that which appears to be our lives, the system of mistaken ideas and values that embody the ego. Kunkel suggests that the way we do this always involves "finding one's place within the service of the we" (Sanford 1984,

152), that is, through commitment to and engagement with others.

Kunkel describes the way in which this is related to surrender to God:

> The emptiness and indifference resulting from the collapse of the Ego and the complete loss of egocentricity enable the individual to discover the very foundations of his life and of human life in general. He sees that man is powerless and important at the same time, that he is part of a larger unit and responsible for it. Furthermore, he realizes—and this is the decisive insight—that he himself as well as the larger unit, the We, is created, sent, supported, endowed, and used by a higher reality who rules the world and in whom he and others live and move and have their being. Thus he feels himself gripped, influenced by God and charged with a concrete task. He feels like a tool seized by a strong hand, or like a knight commissioned by his king. (Sanford 1984, 154)

Kunkel's We-psychology does much to correct the most serious limitations of Jung's view of spirituality while at the same time retaining the richness of his understanding of the dynamics of inner life. Kunkel sees spirituality as self-transcendence and self-surrender, concepts much more central to Christian spirituality than self-fulfillment or individuation.

Existential Psychology

Existential psychology is not so much a specific set of theories or techniques as it is a general approach to psychology. Its beginnings are usually identified with the Danish theologian and philosopher Søren Kierkegaard (1813–1855). It has since evolved into a broad and diverse tradition, so broad that it defies easy definition. Existential approaches stand in opposition to those systems of psychology that view persons reductionistically. Ignoring human essence (the abstraction of traditional psychology), existential psychologists focus on human existence and issues such as the establishment of meaning and purpose for life; freedom, responsibility, and choice; and a creative response to the reality of existential isolation and the inevitability of death.

Søren Kierkegaard

Kierkegaard's breadth as a thinker is reflected in the fact that his books continually cross the boundaries that usually separate literature, psychology, theology, philosophy, and devotional writings. His most influential psychological writings are *Sickness Unto Death* (1849) and *The Concept of Anxiety* (1844). It is here that we find his most extensive discussion of the self and its role in spirituality.

Kierkegaard saw persons as spirit. By this he did not mean that they are immaterial. Rather, "spirit" is the absolute of all that a person can be. Each person is intended to become a self. To Kierkegaard selfhood is not a given, but an achievement. It is to become a self-conscious responsible agent. This is also what it means to be spirit.

"Spirit" is the "self relating to itself" (Kierkegaard 1954, 146). Kierkegaard is here referring to self-acceptance, self-understanding, and self-consciousness, all qualities of a growing self or spirit. But self cannot become all it is intended to be by itself. Ultimately self can only become a true self by relating itself to God (1954, 162). Nordentoft, the major systematizer of Kierkegaard's psychology, describes this aspect of Kierkegaard's thought as follows:

> Man always relates himself to God and man's existence is always determined by this relationship regardless of whether man acknowledges this relationship or not. . . . Man does not become free in an illusory attempt to emancipate himself from every relationship of dependence but by acknowledging to himself his real dependence, that is his createdness by God, and thereby, his relationship to the authority which liberates him. . . . If one does not become free in relationship to the Almighty, one makes oneself un-

free in relation to other powers which one does not know.
(Nordentoft 1972, 89–90)

When the self is dependent on something outside itself
(i.e., God) it can then serve as a point of integration for all
other aspects of personality. In particular, self is the synthesis of elements that are and always will be in opposition
to each other. Self is the synthesis of the finite and the infinite, of the temporal and the eternal, of things possible and
things necessary. These elements are held together by the
self, and because of this, human life involves constant effort, vigilance, and courage to maintain itself as authenti-
cally human.

There is an ever present temptation to let go of the tension. But, according to Kierkegaard this is the coward's
way, as it destroys the self in the effort to escape anxiety.
The result is a one-sidedness to personality, a lack of balance, that inevitably leads to despair. Despair manifests itself in one of two forms: either unwillingness to be one's
own self (despair of weakness) or willingness to be oneself
but in defiance of God (manly despair) (Kierkegaard 1954,
147). In both forms the true self is never fully developed or
realized.

This understanding of spirituality bears striking resemblance to the two positions we considered previously. For
Kierkegaard, as for Jung, self is a synthesis of all parts of
personality, even those that are not easily put together. The
struggle to bring these discrepant parts together is a spiritual struggle by which we become the selves we truly are
rather than living out some false selves.

Also consistent with Jung is Kierkegaard's emphasis on
self-knowledge in this process. Kierkegaard states that
"consciousness of self is the criterion of self. The more
consciousness, the more self" (1954, 162). However, he
makes much more explicit than does Jung the way in
which knowledge of God is a part of this process. Kierkegaard suggests that we begin with a lack of consciousness
of being eternal selves and then come to a knowledge of

this eternal element of our beings. As our selves are defined more and more in the awareness of existing before God, we become our true selves. In Kierkegaard's words, "The more conception of God, the more self; the more self, the more conception of God. Only when the self as this definite individual is conscious of existing before God, only then is it the infinite self" (1954, 211).

Kierkegaard's assertion that self must be grounded in something outside itself and that true selfhood is only possible by being grounded in God is more in line with Kunkel than with Jung. Kierkegaard recognizes the surrender of self to something greater than self, which Kunkel described as being the only path out of egocentricity.

John Finch

John Finch, a contemporary Christian existentialist psychologist, attempts to direct existential psychology back to its roots in Kierkegaard. He notes that existential psychology has largely abandoned any concern for an ultimate reference point of spirit or self and argues that unless spirit is grounded in the Spirit, freedom, responsibility, and all the other transcendent qualities of self are meaningless.

Finch notes that Freudian revisionists such as Adler, Putnam, Jung, and Binswanger all disagreed with Freud's elimination of that aspect of persons which did not fit into his mechanistic and naturalistic model (Malony 1980). They labeled this aspect variously, calling it *spirit*, *soul*, or the *capacity for self-transcendence*, but each held that it is the only source of wholeness. Finch suggests that the human quality observed by these theorists is the *imago Dei*, our imaging of God. He maintains that the term *spirit* is the most suitable for describing this aspect of persons, defining spirit as "that quality which characterizes man as self-transcendent, free, and responsible, and which is unique to man" (Malony 1980, 207).

Viewing spirit as the *imago Dei* suggests to Finch why

we are oriented toward God. This God-likeness, and our orientation toward God, is obscured by a network of defenses that while purporting to protect the self actually suffocates it. These defenses, which Finch calls the "false self," are a result of sin, that is, they are a "sickness created by our egocentric tendency to assert that we are the captains of our fate, the masters of our soul" (Finch and Van Dragt 1985, 375).

Finch's major contribution is his pointing of the way through the false self, back to spirit, and finally to the grounding of spirit in the Spirit. His method is an intensive psychotherapeutic experience conducted within the framework of the traditional spiritual retreat. The process of therapeutic retreat involves a dismantling of the false self and a descent into the dread, which the mystics have called the "abyss." Finch describes the experience as "a radical and ineffable confrontation with one's own being which becomes at the same instant an experience of the infinite love of God. For, having abandoned one's feeble attempts to constitute one's own security, one finds that he or she is and always has been held" (1985, 377).

The goal of Finch's Christian existential psychotherapy is to encourage persons seeking help to find and develop their true selves, their spirits. Finch describes this as a spiritual encounter, wherein the therapist attempts to "excavate and probe through the years of rationalized encrustations; lovingly appealing to the individual's carefully concealed sense of responsibility; fanning the little sparks of conscience back to flame; uncluttering the conscience and attempting to witness of the Spirit to the spirit . . . to encourage the spirit to emerge and be itself" (Malony 1980, 183).

Finch's therapy is reminiscent of Kunkel's emphasis on the necessity of crisis in the breakdown of egocentricity. For both Kunkel and Finch spiritual growth necessarily involves crisis. The encrustations of the false self are not broken through easily, but until they are, true self (spirit) does not emerge. Finch also shares with Kunkel the notion that the enemy of spirituality is ego-centeredness. Both also affirm that only self-transcendence that is rooted in God can produce the wholeness of personality that we need.

Adrian van Kaam

The final representative of the existential tradition whom we shall consider is Adrian van Kaam. Trained as both a psychologist and a Catholic priest, van Kaam has frequently focused on issues of spirituality and the way in which psychology can inform or assist spiritual growth.

Van Kaam's clearest statement on spirituality and psychology is found in his book *On Being Yourself*. Here he studies the relationship between spiritual growth and self-discovery. His major thesis is that spirituality is a person's attempt to integrate oneself in the light of one's presence with God (van Kaam 1972, 25). By this he means we should always be aware of being in the presence of God and should integrate the various aspects of personality in the light of this awareness.

According to van Kaam, the spiritual quest is the quest for self-discovery and fulfillment. It is the quest for the real me, the original me. However, this is not to be confused with self-enhancement or mere ego fulfillment. It is not to be a search for self in isolation from God but a search for self-in-God. This is the difference between self-ism as idolatry and Christian spiritual growth.

Van Kaam argues that when Scripture speaks of giving up of self or of denying self, it should not be interpreted as losing our identities or fusing with the Godhead. Rather, it means that "I should distance myself from false self-images. I should not pursue after an isolated God-like self" (1972, 7). The search is for our original selves hidden in God, and only then do we find our true selves.

Although Christian spirituality means looking to God to

find meaning and the point of integration, this point of integration is not primarily exterior; rather, it is interior. Van Kaam describes the spiritual life as a life of inner direction, a life lived in contact with our deepest selves. It is here that we find the most personal statement of God's will for our lives. It is here that we learn whom God calls us as unique individuals to be. And what we discover is that each of us is called to be a unique self, an original creation.

According to van Kaam, true spirituality excludes mere imitation or conformity. A person's spiritual life can never be a carbon copy of another's. Christianity has often missed this central truth, assuming that as we become more like Christ we become more similar to each other. Van Kaam asserts that this is a fundamental error, for the more we grow in Christ, the more we should find and express the uniqueness of Christ in us.

Spiritual persons are characterized by direction and purpose in their lives. These are not superficial or arbitrary directions and meanings; rather, they flow out from the center of personality. In contrast, nonspiritual persons may also have direction and meaning, but these do not flow out of their innermost selves. Christian spirituality flows out of a union with Christ. In van Kaam's words, "Spirituality in the most profound sense resides in the core of my being, in my deepest self or spirit, where I as willing unite my will to the will of God for me" (1972, 54).

Van Kaam's understanding of mature spirituality resulting in meaning and direction flowing out of the depths of personality is akin to Jung's differentiation between true and false spirituality. Both Jung and van Kaam see true spirituality as beginning with integrated interiority and moving toward meaningfully directed behavior. Van Kaam's view of spirituality also helps us understand the role of self-discovery in spiritual growth. When we pursue our selves in the presence of God we are able to find our true and original spiritual selves, which will forever elude us if we pursue self-fulfillment apart from God.

Contemplative Psychology

Gerald May

Drawing particularly on the wisdom of the ancient contemplatives of both Western and Eastern spiritual traditions, Gerald May has suggested the contours of a psychology that relies on intuition while continuing to respect other traditional modes of knowing, such as observation and logical inference. He suggests that the goal of contemplative psychology is not to solve mystery but to appreciate it, to seek to know, experience, love, and nurture it even without understanding it (May 1982, 30). Contemplative psychology draws its name from contemplative spirituality, which May defines as "the willingness and courage to open oneself to mystery" (1982, 32).

Basic to May's discussion of the attitudes behind a contemplative approach to psychology or spirituality is the distinction he draws between willingness and willfulness. Willingness he defines as surrender to a reality greater than oneself and relinquishment of the idea that a person can actually master life. As such it is a surrender of separateness. Willfulness is the setting apart of oneself from the deepest reality in an attempt to master one's own destiny and control or manipulate existence. In brief, "willingness is saying yes to the mystery of being alive in each moment. Willfulness is saying no, or perhaps more commonly, 'Yes but ...' " (1982, 6).

The relationship between spirituality and mystery is important for May.

> Spirit and mystery are closely related. ... Mystery may not always be spiritual but there is no doubt that spirituality is always mysterious. . . . The search for an experiential appreciation of the meaning of life is a spiritual quest and if it is followed deeply enough it will inevitably come upon mystery. (1982, 32)

Religion and spirituality are also closely related.

> Religion can exist without spirituality if it consists only of standards of conduct, nonexperiential theology and rituals that are practiced for no felt reason. . . . A spiritual quest becomes decidedly religious only when one begins to identify a relationship with the Ultimate Spirit or Mystery and when that relationship begins to manifest itself in specific behaviors such as worship. . . . No spiritual quest can progress very far without becoming religious (1982, 32–33).

The keystone of contemplative spirituality is what May calls "the unitive experience." This is the experience of a momentary loss of self-definition accompanied by some degree of self-transcendence. In these moments, all mental activity seems to be temporarily suspended and the person feels caught up in a state of awe or wonder, and possibly fear or anxiety. However, there is also a pervasive sense of being-at-one. Unitive experiences appear to be a universal spiritual phenomenon. May reports that when interviewed in depth and asked the right questions, virtually everyone can report one or two such experiences (1982, 54).

These experiences are important for spirituality in that they clearly exemplify the difference between willingness and willfulness. Unitive experiences cannot be willfully produced; they can only be willingly accepted. They are a gift of grace. As such they illustrate the surrender that characterizes genuine spiritual experience.

In its most basic form, May says, the spiritual quest is a search for our roots, "not the roots of family, nor of race, nor even of the human species, but our roots as creatures of and in this cosmos" (1982, 89). Human spiritual longing is realizing that we have forgotten who we are, accepting that, and searching for our place. May points out that psychology can in no way address this kind of quest without reducing it to some kind of meeting of needs, a narcissistic view of the process. Only religion can help us understand such spiritual questing. Then we understand "that the frenzy of searching is not really needed, that in fact we have already been found" (1982, 89). Searching will usually continue, but searching eventually comes to be superseded by surrender. May continues:

> The [spiritual] longing hovers around the edges of daily awareness, kept alive by occasional spiritual experiences and momentary recollections of the "home" that existed before self-definition and independent identity were established. The longing for re-union with this "home" is marginally available to awareness but most of the time we are so preoccupied with other issues that we fail to notice it. (1982, 91)

William McNamara

While William McNamara does not label his work *contemplative psychology*, his writing is similar to that of May. Drawing his psychological insights from the realm of Christian mysticism, McNamara defines the goal of Christian spirituality as the realization of union with God (McNamara 1975, 399). He argues that in this alone lies the ultimate fulfillment of human personality; this is the answer to life's deepest yearnings.

Of particular importance is McNamara's discussion of the deep center of personality. Is it spirit, or is it Spirit? He answers:

> The center of the soul is not God, but it is so intimately grounded in God that it can and sometimes is mistaken for God himself. The center is the created ground of being grounded in God's Uncreated Being. . . . This most profound and sacred depth of the soul is the dwelling place of God. It is in this divine center that we are made in his likeness. Nothing can fill or satisfy this center except God himself. At this center God is more real than man is (1972, 405).

Drawing on the richness of Christian mysticism, McNamara and May offer us a perspective of spirituality that is compatible with and at the same time enriches the perspectives of the other theorists considered in this chapter. Once again we are shown spirituality as being deep longings that can ultimately only be fulfilled in self-transcendence. Humans in and of themselves are incomplete. Our deepest yearnings drive us beyond ourselves for their fulfillment. These yearnings are usually called spiritual yearnings, because their satisfaction requires that we transcend the ordinary modes of life. They call us to something higher and yet something deeper at the same time. They call us into the depths of ourselves, and yet they call us out and beyond ourselves. These are the mysteries of spiritual longings.

This review of several of the systems of psychology that address spirituality demonstrates that spirituality does not need to stand outside the domain of psychology. Spiritual longings occur within the very heart of personality; they are not the stirrings of something independent of the rest of personality. They can, therefore, be studied psychologically. Even if this point of reference does not afford a complete understanding of spirituality, it does contribute to our understanding of its nature and place within personality.

There is a surprising degree of consensus among the theorists whom we have reviewed about the nature of spirituality. All seem to agree that spirituality is associated with an integration of interior life (ideally including all the diverse aspects of personality) and external behavior. Also, they agree that this includes moving beyond the false selves that we create and then confuse with our true selves. With the exception of Jung, all agree that the transcendence of false selves and the integration of personality can only occur when the self is dependent on God. Only when self, or spirit, is grounded in the Spirit, do we find our true selves-in-God. The spiritual quest is, therefore, our quest for our places and for our identities, a quest that may not appear overtly spiritual, but one that is indeed spiritual given what these theorists assert to be the only satisfactory solution to the quest.

But how does this understanding of spirituality relate to historic Christian understandings of spirituality? When we approach the topic, not from the perspective of psychology but from that of Christianity, what is it that we find? It is to this matter that we now turn.

4

Christian Spirituality

Even a cursory examination of the history of Christian spirituality reveals the fact that there is no single Christian definition of spirituality. In fact, this history is sometimes interpreted as a history of spiritualities. However, it may be more accurate to say that there are not different spiritualities but rather different ways of experiencing and expressing the reality of God.

The essence of Christian spirituality is the experience of God. Later in this chapter we will add several other definitive characteristics of spirituality. First and foremost, however, Christian spirituality is a deep relationship with God made possible by the indwelling presence of the Holy Spirit. Here the human spirit is grounded in the Holy Spirit and experiences intimacy and mystical union with God.

Spiritual growth, then, is growth into an ever deeper and closer relationship with God. In this relationship our wills and characters are increasingly conformed to God's will and character, and we become more whole. Contrary to some caricatures of Christian spirituality, as we grow spiritually we do not become less human. Rather, we discover our humanity; we become more truly and fully human. We Christians assert that in our relationship with God we find our true selves. As we come home to our

Creator-Redeemer-God we find where we belong and who we are. Spiritual growth is thus closely related to psychological growth. To grow into a deeper relationship with God is to find our human identity and to discover a point of reference for the integration of our personality.

Christians throughout the ages have not agreed about the means of such spiritual growth. To Roman Catholics the means of grace have been the seven sacraments: baptism, confirmation, the Eucharist, reconciliation, matrimony, anointing of the sick, and ordination to Holy Orders. Protestants have accepted only two sacraments, baptism and the Eucharist, and in addition have emphasized the Word of God as the other essential means of grace. While not formally classifying it as a means of grace, both Protestants and Roman Catholics have also considered prayer to be central to spiritual growth.

Ways of Experiencing God

In his book *A History of Christian Spirituality* Holmes points out that the variety of ways in which Christians have learned to experience God can be placed in relationship to two bipolar scales: a kataphatic/apophatic scale and a speculative/affective scale (Holmes 1980, 4). The first scale describes techniques of spiritual growth, while the second describes the primary effect of these techniques on the spiritual life.

The terms *kataphatic* and *apophatic* refer to the two classic approaches to meditation. Kataphatic spirituality is based on the active use of the imagination. The Christian identifies positive images of God and uses these images as a tool for meditation. For example, meditation might take the form of visualizing Christ as the good shepherd. Additional details in this image could include his carrying a wounded sheep or his searching the lonely hills for a lost one. The meditator may also try to hear the sounds on the hillside, feel the coolness of the mountain air, or experience the hunger of the self-sacrificing shepherd, thus involving as many of the senses as possible.

Other images of God that could be used in kataphatic meditation are God as light, as fire, as heavenly Father, or as bridegroom. Christian traditions that have been most closely identified with kataphatic spirituality are medieval monastics (Gregory the Great), fourteenth-century mystics (Richard Rolle; Julian of Norwich), and sixteenth-century Spanish mystics (Ignatius of Loyola; Teresa of Avila; John of the Cross).

In contrast to the kataphatic method, apophatic spirituality is an "emptying" technique. Instead of focusing on images that symbolize some aspect of God, the apophatic approach emphasizes what God is not. God is not merely a heavenly Father; he is much much more than this. Nor is he well-represented by the imagery of the shepherd. These, and all other images, are judged to be imperfect and dangerous misrepresentations of his being. In the apophatic tradition God is encountered as mystery. He is the hidden God who, while having revealed himself to us, is still only encountered in obscure awareness. While kataphatic spirituality affirms the knowability of God and the intimacy that humans can have with him, apophatic spirituality warns of the dangers of glib overfamiliarity and the idolatrous assumption that the reality of God can be captured in words or symbols.

The goal of apophatic spirituality is to experience union with God. What is discovered in this experience with God is not so much knowledge as love. God is found to be incomprehensible to our intellects but not to our love. Examples of this tradition include Eastern Orthodox spirituality, Meister Eckhart, and *The Cloud of Unknowing*.

The speculative/affective scale is the second dimension suggested by Holmes (1980) for understanding the variety of ways in which Christians approach God and expect to meet him in their lives. Speculative approaches to spirituality are those traditions that emphasize the illumination of the mind (or intellect), while affective approaches emphasize illumination of the heart (or emotions).

In speculative spirituality God is encountered with the mind, resulting in a rational and propositional theology. Speculative spirituality is characteristic of Eastern Orthodox Christianity and most Western Protestant Christianity. It is developed most clearly by Reformed (Calvinist) Christians who affirm the importance of knowing God through his self-revelation in Scripture. In this tradition God is not primarily found in some nonrational or emotional experience. Rather, he is encountered with the mind and is known through the study of his Word, the Bible. Speculative spirituality tends to emphasize theology to the neglect of mystical intimacy with God.

In affective spirituality God is met in the heart rather than in the head. Merely knowing about God is judged to be a poor substitute for a personal relationship. Examples of such a "heart religion" can be found in the whole history of Christianity, ranging from the early desert fathers of the fourth and fifth centuries to modern-day charismatics, both Roman Catholic and Protestant. In all its manifestations, affective spirituality emphasizes the experience with God to the neglect of theology or systematic reflection on that experience. When doctrine is present, it focuses on the nonrational aspects of the experience with God.

It should be noted that the distinction between head and heart in the second dimension of Holmes's model may be artificial and even misleading. In his book *Spirituality and Human Emotions* Roberts (1983) argues that emotions are matters of both head and heart. Along with others Roberts maintains that feelings are closely related to thoughts, and therefore, the attempt to classify experiences as being either in the head or in the heart is to confuse the issue. This is in fact borne out by the examples of the speculative/affective dimension in the above paragraphs. Eastern Orthodox Christianity is not devoid of emotion, and Calvin certainly had a religion of both heart and head. Thus, while attempts to classify spiritual experience by such a dichotomy are common, the dangers of such distinctions should be kept in mind.

Holmes does acknowledge that the two scales are closely interrelated (see fig. 1). It is difficult to describe functioning on one scale without reference to the other. Holmes suggests that full-orbed spirituality ideally contains a balance of all four ways of knowing God, as represented by the circle in the center of the figure. Problems in spirituality occur when one moves outside this circle of balance. Holmes lists four specific dangers resulting from such loss of balance. Rationalism results from an exaggerated speculative/kataphatic spirituality, pietism from exaggerated kataphatic/affective spirituality, quietism from exaggerated apophatic/affective spirituality, and encratism (extreme ascetism) from exaggerated speculative/apophatic spirituality.

Fig. 1.*   **Ways of Experiencing God**

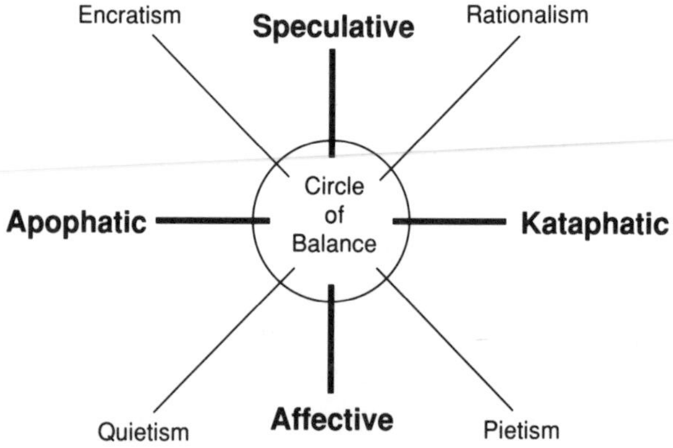

*Taken from *A History of Christian Spirituality* (New York: Seabury, 1980). Used by permission.

The goal of this chapter is not to review either the definitions or the history of Christian spirituality. The former task is too abstract and would not help us really understand Christian spirituality, and the latter task would draw us too far from our focus. The more modest objective is to suggest the breadth of experience encompassed within Christian spirituality by presenting several historical examples. The selection necessarily reflects personal bias. However, by looking at some ways in which Christians have understood and experienced their spirituality, we should be in a better position to develop a psychological perspective on the spiritual aspects of persons.

Desert Spirituality

From pre-Christian times the desert has been the place of meeting God. It was in the desert that Moses received the revelation of God's name (Exod. 3:2). While they were in the desert God gave the Ten Commandments to the children of Israel. It was natural, therefore, for early Christians to turn to the desert when seeking spiritual renewal, and since that time the desert, both literally and metaphorically, has been a constant theme in Christian spirituality.

The literal practice of desert spirituality peaked in the fourth and fifth centuries A.D. During this period as many as twenty thousand people lived alone or in monastic groups in the deserts of Egypt, Syria, and Palestine, and thousands more visited them for spiritual counsel (Edwards 1980, 50). Desert spirituality involved a fiery and intense love of God. The desert fathers frequently described the presence of God as a "fire of love." To be in God's presence was to have a fire lit within the soul, a fire that would burn up the passions and possessiveness of the heart and allow the individual to respond with love. This fire of love would also warm the soul, a warmth often reported by desert mystics as being a physical sensation.

Desert spirituality emphasizes solitude, renunciation, spiritual purgation, self-knowledge, and self-control. The desert was the place to overcome illusions, gain spiritual discernment, and purify desire. This spirituality was one of radical commitment—commitment to the martyrdom of the false self and the first-hand direct experience of God.

Prayer was critical to the spiritual work of the desert. John Cassian (A.D. 360–435), the most systematic of the desert teachers, recommended silent prayer based upon the repetition of short verses of Scripture. Although the Jesus Prayer ("Lord Jesus Christ, Son of God, have mercy upon me, a sinner") is most closely identified with the Russian Orthodox Church, its earliest use was by the desert fathers. Other desert fathers, most notably Evagrius Ponticus (A.D. 346–399), took a more apophatic approach to prayer. To him even the contemplation of Scripture was a block to the emptying of the mind, which he considered necessary for prayer.

Marcarius described the desert fathers as "men intoxicated with God" (Leech 1977, 142). Their experience with God was direct and their response to him was deeply affective. On the kataphatic/apophatic scale desert spirituality was balanced, with elements of both being present. There was, however, little hint of a speculative (rationalistic) approach to Christian experience. Desert spirituality exemplifies the deep affective response to God that is possible when we encounter him directly and personally.

Eastern Orthodox Spirituality

Eastern Orthodox spirituality, while distinguished from that of the desert, is continuous with and inseparable from it. From the desert the Eastern Church took the tradition of apophatic prayer and developed it into the distinctive Eastern tradition of *hesychasm*. Derived from *hēsychia*, the Greek word for "quietness" or "stillness," in the most general sense *hesychasm* refers to quiet inner prayer. It is prayer free of images and concepts, free from thought. It is an apophatic approach to prayer that emphasizes emptying as preparation for receiving. In the narrow sense *hesychasm* refers to using the Jesus Prayer, particularly when used along with controlled breathing.

The Jesus Prayer can take one of several forms. Its most complete form is "Lord Jesus Christ, Son of God, have mercy upon me, a sinner." Often the prayer is shortened, the most succinct version being the simple uttering of the name *Jesus*. This reveals the true essence of prayer, the invocation of the name of Jesus. In the Old Testament, Jews expressed their reverence for the name of God by never saying the divine name aloud. The name of the Most High was considered too profound to be spoken. The power of the name of Jesus is a pervasive New Testament theme that builds upon this awareness. Devils are cast out and people are healed and justified by the name of Jesus. Jesus also instructed his followers to pray in his name and told them that "whatsoever you ask in my name, that will I do" (John 14:13). Furthermore, Paul attests to the power of the Name by asserting that "at the name of Jesus every knee shall bow" (Phil. 2:10). It is this biblical reverence for the Name that forms the foundation of the Jesus Prayer.

Kallistos Ware points out that the significance of the Jesus Prayer lies not only in the power of the name of Jesus, but also in the prayer's theological and devotional completeness (Ware 1974, 8–9). Theologically, the prayer contains a succinct summary of the two chief mysteries of the Christian faith, the incarnation and the Trinity. It calls to mind the two natures of Christ, for he is called by his human name *Jesus* and by his divine name *Son of God*. His sonship also points to the Father, and the presence of the Holy Spirit is attested to by the fact that no one can say "Lord Jesus" except by the Holy Spirit (1 Cor. 12:3). Devotionally the prayer is no less comprehensive. It includes both the posture of adoration, as we address him as "Lord Jesus Christ, Son of God," and the posture of penitence or confession, as we recall our dependence upon God's mercy for the forgiveness of our sins. As such, the Jesus Prayer contains the whole gospel in summary.

The intent of the Jesus Prayer is to move from verbal prayer to mental prayer to inward prayer, or prayer of the heart. The goal is not to meditate upon the words of the prayer but through repetition to allow the prayer to descend into the depths of our beings; it will then emerge as a prayer not of our minds but of our spirits. It thus becomes a prayer welling up within ourselves apart from a conscious effort to pray.

The repetition of the Jesus Prayer allows a person to move from *offering* a prayer to *becoming* a prayer. This is the meaning of the New Testament injunction to pray without ceasing (1 Thess. 5:17). Our whole lives are to become prayers. We are to become more and more aware of ourselves as standing in God's presence and thus learn to make our whole lives responses to him.

The use of breathing exercises with the Jesus Prayer aids in making the prayer a response from the depths of the heart. Only if the body, too, is involved in prayer can prayer truly be the response of the whole person. This is why bowing, kneeling, and prostrating one's self are so important to the Christian's prayer life.

Although the specific breathing exercises may take different forms, one common one has been to silently repeat the first phrase of the prayer upon inhalation ("Lord Jesus Christ, Son of God") and the second upon exhalation ("Have mercy upon me, a sinner"). This is then often shortened to the silent pronouncement of "Lord Jesus Christ" or "Lord Jesus" as each breath is drawn in, and "Have mercy upon me" as the breath is released. By repeated practice, this prayer can become a conditioned response to the breathing, a prayer surging up from the depths of the heart apart from any conscious efforts to pray.

One profound account of an experience with the Jesus Prayer is found in *The Way of a Pilgrim* (French 1965). This is the spiritual diary of a nineteenth-century Russian who,

upon the death of his wife, left everything behind and committed himself to a life of wandering and prayer. Walking
the length of Russia several times he set as his goal the cul-
tivation of what he called "ceaseless prayer of the heart."
He generally avoided towns and villages, approaching
them only when his supply of dry crusts or water ran low.
The rest of the days, months, and years he spent walking
and repeating the Jesus Prayer.

At first, prayer for this pilgrim was verbal. It then became a mental prayer, uttered without verbalization. And
finally it came to be a prayer of the heart. After a day in a
town providing spiritual counsel to others or conversing in
the marketplace, he would begin to feel pressure within as
the prayer welled up seeking release. He then set out once
again and immediately was lost in the rapturous enjoy-
ment of the presence of God. Meanwhile, the prayer continued, bubbling up into his consciousness without effort.
He reported that the prayer could coexist with other conscious thoughts. Similar experiences are reported by
others seasoned in using prayer of the heart. They need not
actively try to pray or try to refrain from thinking about
other things. Once the prayer has become a prayer of the
heart, it unfolds as a continuous offering of the person's
spirit.

The power of the Jesus Prayer is not in the mechanical
repetition of certain words. Christian prayer is not a talis-
man. The Jesus Prayer, like any Christian prayer, is an
expression of a heart attitude, that is, a heart oriented
toward God in faith. Nor is the prayer just a means to relax
or even to concentrate, although both may be by-products.
The prayer is "an invocation specifically addressed to another person—to God-made-man, Jesus Christ, our personal Savior and Redeemer" (Ware, 1974, 22). Ware goes
on to say that it is not an isolated technique, but has meaning and propriety only within the context of personal faith.
He asserts that "the invocation of the Name presupposes
that the one who says the prayer believes in Jesus Christ as
Son of God and Savior. Behind the repetition of a form of

words there must exist a living faith in the Lord Jesus—in who He is and in what He has done for me personally" (1974, 22).

A central feature of Eastern Orthodox spirituality is the apophatic approach to God. For Gregory of Nyssa all concepts about God are idols. "One does not know God except in terms of our incapacity to apprehend him" (Leech 1977, 143). The spiritual path necessarily involves moving beyond belief in the knowability of God to humble acceptance of the way of ignorance, the way of faith. But Orthodox spirituality is not, as this might suggest, anti-intellectual or antitheological. It is, as we have already seen, strongly theological and biblical. With the exception of the Book of Revelation, the whole New Testament is read each year in the Orthodox divine liturgy. Furthermore, the Eastern Church strongly believes that Scripture should illumine understanding and guide behavior. As Evagrius says, "If you are a theologian, you will pray truly. And if you pray truly, you are a theologian" (Lash 1983, 283). This quotation also reveals the unity of theology and spirituality that characterizes Orthodox spirituality.

Other important aspects of Orthodox spirituality are the motifs of witness and martyrdom, the strong quality of asceticism, its christocentric mysticism, and its deep liturgical and ecclesiastical commitments. Although the tradition encourages private prayer, it teaches that the main source of an individual's spiritual strength comes from the corporate liturgical worship of the church. This anti-individualistic view of the process of spiritual growth common to Eastern Orthodox churches is summarized in the saying that "no one is saved alone, he is saved in the Church, as a member of it and in union with all its other members" (Lash 1983, 285).

Orthodox spirituality is for the most part an apophatic/ speculative spirituality. Its goal is union with God. This does not refer to a pantheistic fusion but rather to a sharing of God's life through divine grace. To the tradition of

affective spirituality associated with the desert, Eastern
Orthodoxy adds the illumination of the mind. Furthermore, as a corrective against an overly rationalistic spirituality, it emphasizes the mystery and unknowability of
God. God is bigger than any of our ideas about him and we
are to approach him humbly, mistrusting the adequacy of
our conceptions of him.

Roman Catholic Spirituality

Roman Catholicism of the past four centuries provides
us with several significant illustrations of Christian spirituality. The first and perhaps most important formative
influence on contemporary Catholic spirituality was that
of the Spanish mystics. Ignatius of Loyola (1491–1556) was
the founder of the Jesuits, and Teresa of Avila (1515–1582)
and John of the Cross (1542–1591) were Carmelite reformers. Holmes describes this group's contribution as
"the first science of the spiritual life" (Holmes 1980, 93).
By this he refers to their systematic analysis of the totality
of spiritual experience, with their intention to describe
both the means and the ends of that experience in an objective manner.

Ignatius's most famous and enduring work is his *Spiritual Exercises*. Here he sets out his guidelines for spiritual
growth in the form of a series of exercises based upon
meditations on the life of Christ. These emphasize kataphatic imagination as the mode of meditation and also
make extensive use of examination of conscience, contemplation, and vocal and mental prayer. Ignatius utilizes all
the classical faculties of the mind (memory, understanding, and will) and each of the five senses, systematically involving each in the work of prayer and meditation. Thus,
for example, the Christian might take an image such as the
trial of Jesus and apply each of the five senses to that
image as a means of meditation. This would be followed by
recollection of what is known of the actual incident, what

is understood to have been its significance, and resolutions for the future that grow out of this meditation. The exercise would then culminate with prayer for grace to keep these resolutions.

Ignatian spirituality places great emphasis on freedom, particularly the freedom to choose. This and his emphasis on self-knowledge as a route to this freedom have led a number of authors to compare the methods of Ignatius to those of psychoanalysis and other depth psychologies (Barnhouse 1975). Christotherapy, an approach to the integration of psychotherapy and spiritual guidance developed by Tyrrell (1982) and described in chapter 7, is based on the *Spiritual Exercises,* indicating the rich potential for psychospiritual growth and healing contained within Ignatian spirituality.

Teresa of Avila, the Carmelite reformer, was a remarkable mystic and teacher of the life of prayer. On the whole her spirituality was kataphatic, involving a rich use of the imagination. She built her spiritual theology around images arising from her mystical experiences, which were often of a strongly sexual nature. In *Interior Castle* she describes the seven "rooms" of the "castle of the soul" (Teresa of Avila 1972). These rooms represent growth in grace from a position of love of the world to spiritual marriage. The last three rooms correspond to progressively deeper and deeper stages of union with God, an experience Teresa describes as "drenching rain."

Teresa's spirituality is immensely practical. She asserts that the Lord is to be found among the saucepans and in the menial tasks of the day. Furthermore, she argues that both contemplation and the menial tasks of life constitute service of God, and that one is not higher in value than the other.

John of the Cross is, with Teresa of Avila, one of the giants in the history of Christian spirituality. More apophatic and speculative than Teresa of Avila, his spirituality was primarily characterized by a profoundly biblical orientation. Often identified as an important force in the

Catholic Counter-Reformation, John was clear about the central place of justification by faith in spiritual growth. He described the faith by which we come to God as "dark faith," meaning that faith is the act of being satisfied with what we cannot understand.

Developing this imagery further, John says that the path of spiritual growth necessarily leads one through personal crisis, an experience he calls "the dark night of the soul." This is not something to be avoided; rather, is it our divine appointment with the grace of God. Usually following a period of spiritual progress, entry into the dark night of the soul is characterized by depression, spiritual dryness, the inability to pursue the spiritual disciplines, and a great desire to give up the spiritual pilgrimage. However, John urges us not to despair.

> When you see your appetites darkened, your inclinations dry and constrained, your faculties incapacitated for any interior exercise, do not be afflicted; think on this as a grace, since God is freeing you from yourself and taking from you your own activity. . . . God takes you by the hand and guides you in darkness, as though you were blind, along a way and to a place you know not. You would never have succeeded in reaching this place no matter how good your eyes and your feet. (John of the Cross 1964, 365)

The waters where John leads us are deep and troubled. However, we cannot avoid them if we are to make significant progress in the spiritual life. He assures us that they are not waters of destruction but of liberation. It is for this reason that he urges us to embrace the darkness as grace. He describes his own embrace of the dark night of the soul in the following lines:

> O guiding night!
> O night more lovely than the dawn!
> O night that has united
> The lover with His beloved,
> Transforming the beloved in her Lover. (1964, 296)

Here he shows us the ultimate purpose of the dark night: self-transformation and union with God.

The seventeenth-century French bishop Frances de Sales (1567–1622) sought to combine Ignatian and Carmelite spirituality, the result being an approach to meditation that has had wide and continuing appeal. As presented in *Introduction to the Devout Life* (de Sales 1950), Salesian meditation consists of five steps:

1. Preparation:
   Place yourself in the presence of God.
   Pray for assistance.
   Imagine a scene from the life of Jesus.
2. Consideration:
   Identify those images in the scene that affect you.
3. Affections and resolutions:
   Convert feelings into understandings and then into resolutions.
4. Conclusion:
   Thanksgiving.
   Oblation or offering of the results for meditation.
   Petition to fulfill in this day your insights.
5. The spiritual nosegay:*
   That which we carry through the day from the meditation (Holmes 1980, 106).

Sales's teachings were strongly affective and apophatic and eventually led to the heresy of quietism—the quest for complete passivity and annihilation of the will, a teaching of Francis Fenelon (1651–1715) and Miguel de Molinos (1628–1696).

Post-Vatican II Roman Catholic spirituality has a renewed emphasis on the Holy Spirit as the one who gives

*The "spiritual nosegay" reveals the gentleness of Sales's spirituality. A nosegay was a bunch of sweet smelling flowers that ladies and gentlemen of the period carried with them when they went outdoors so they would not be overcome by the stench of open sewers. This was Sales's image of the aftereffect of meditation, a sweet aroma that freshens the day.

Christians new life by incorporating them into the death and resurrection of Jesus Christ. Dominic Maruca describes this renewal as follows: "Spirituality is in the first instance living in the Spirit; systematic reflection and interpretation of that lived experience is spirituality in a secondary sense" (Maruca 1983, 337). Flowing out of this is the conviction that spirituality is a life of deep faith that coordinates contemplative love of God and political love of neighbor. Thus, contemporary Roman Catholicism has witnessed renewed interest in the liturgy, spiritual retreats, spiritual guidance, and other spiritual disciplines, and extensive promotion of social justice. The result is a spirituality that reestablishes its connections with the best in the church's past while simultaneously situating itself at the heart of modern life's economic, social, and political tensions.

Reformation Spirituality

Louis Bouyer begins the section on Protestant spirituality in his three-volume classic, *A History of Christian Spirituality,* with the assertion that nothing is more difficult to describe than Protestant spirituality (Bouyer 1965, 57). He explains that this is principally due to the Protestant mistrust of mysticism. The depths of the Protestant aversion even to the word *spirituality* is reflected in the fact that most Protestant Bible and theology dictionaries fail to include an article on spirituality. Out of a desire to eliminate the overtones of spiritual introspection and in order to emphasize personal commitment to Christ and a life of obedience to the Word of God, Protestants have tended to prefer such terms as *holiness* or *godliness* to describe the spiritual state. To describe the Christian's attitude toward God, Protestants have tended to use the term *devotion.*

The Reformers themselves were not afraid of the language of spirituality. Martin Luther (1483–1546) was a son of the German monastic tradition. He read the mystics, especially Eckhart and Tauler, and twice published a truncated manuscript of a fourteenth-century mystical treatise called *Theologica Germanica*. Luther said of this book that, apart from the Bible and Augustine, no book had taught him more about God and about the human condition (Holmes 1980, 125). Later in life Luther became less mystical, and his prayer life became more practical and simple.

Luther's understanding of and personal practice of prayer clearly reveals the depth of his spirituality. In a letter written in 1535 to his barber and best friend, Peter Beskendorf, Luther set out his advice for the development of personal prayer (Luther 1968). Luther encouraged praying the Lord's Prayer, the Ten Commandments, and if time and energy allowed, the Apostles' Creed. Luther encouraged his friend to reflect on each separate phrase from four perspectives. First he should take the phrase as an instruction or a command. Then he should turn it into a matter for thanksgiving, a confession, and finally a petition. However, Luther warned that Beskendorf should not follow his specific words, but should rather use them as a *pattern* for personal prayer.

Describing the Lord's Prayer, Luther wrote:

> I suckle at the Lord's Prayer like a child, and as an old man eat and drink from it and never get my fill. It is the very best prayer.... What a great pity that the prayer of such a master is prattled and chattered so irreverently all over the world! How many pray the Lord's Prayer several thousand times in the course of a year, and if they were to keep on doing so for a thousand years they would not have tasted nor prayed one iota, one dot, of it! (1968, 200).

Luther's contributions to Christian spirituality were profound. Bouyer notes that the most significant was that he reintroduced a piety directly inspired by the Bible and diffused it among the common people in a manner unknown since the patristic times (Bouyer 1965, 71). This tremendous spread of personal piety was related to his doctrine of the priesthood of all believers, a teaching that made the serious pursuit of spirituality a concern for all Christians. Furthermore, his doctrines of justification by faith alone and of Scripture (God's personal revelation to each believer) were significant forces in shaping the biblical and God-centered qualities of Protestant spirituality.

John Calvin (1509–1564) was trained as a lawyer and was self-taught in theology. Raised with something of a contempt for all things clerical, he was never sympathetic toward the Catholic tradition. Calvin rejected pilgrimages, fasting, and other ascetic practices. He, more than Luther, gave classic Protestant spirituality its distinctive speculative (rationalistic) and kataphatic character. Prayer became a matter not so much of contemplation as of dialogue.

Calvin's writings did, however, make rich use of images. He liked to describe the relationship of Christ with the believer in terms of the image of marriage. He was also not afraid to speak of the union of God and the believer. In fact, he argued that the purpose of sanctification is ultimately just such a union. This union is attained when we are grafted into Christ and formed according to him as our exemplar. This union is not absorption, but rather a participation in his life, made possible by the Holy Spirit. It involves communion at the deepest level of our beings, not merely a harmony of wills.

Lucien Joseph Richard in *The Spirituality of John Calvin* says that the major themes of Calvin's spirituality are "knowledge of God and man; the necessity of honoring the glory of God, demanding, on the part of man, faith, service and obedience; total dependence upon God's word incarnated in Christ, and the practical attitude of man expressed in piety and worship" (Richard 1974, 99). For Calvin, piety is grounded in dependence upon God and his Word and is revealed in worship and service. The pious person is the person who has taken his or her place within God's order and who expresses devotion to God in obedience to his Word.

The central place given to God's sovereignty and his glory are an important part of Calvinist spirituality. It enriches worship and secures spirituality as a God-centered state. The grandeur of Calvin's vision of God's glory makes his iconoclasm understandable. Anything that comes between God and man (be this a picture, statue, or symbol) is at risk of becoming an idol in that it blocks the perception of God's glory.

Calvin's doctrine of sanctification made an important contribution to Protestant spirituality. This doctrine complemented Luther's doctrine of justification. It retained the gratuity of salvation while adding the importance of the transformation of a person's whole life. This transformation is spiritual growth. Without a doctrine of sanctification Protestants would have been left without a theological basis for spirituality.

The Reformers introduced a spirituality of personal piety grounded in the Scriptures and revealed in acts of worship, obedience, and service. Associated with this biblical grounding was their insistence on preaching as a means of spiritual nourishment, which became one of the enduring distinctions of Protestant spirituality.

Pietist Spirituality

Pietism is a misunderstood tradition within Christianity. As a common noun, the word generally refers to an experiential tradition within the history of Christian spirituality that emphasizes the practicalities of the Christian life. As such, this tradition was present from the days of the apostles. Stoeffler (*The Rise of Evangelical Pietism*, 1971) interprets the word this way, and says that, in addition to its being practical and experiential, other defining characteristics of pietism are its biblical focus, its perfectionistic bent, and its reforming interest (Stoeffler 1971, 9–23).

As a proper noun, Pietism refers specifically to a late

sixteenth- and seventeenth-century movement in Germany. This movement was a reaction to the sterile theology of Lutheranism. In its place it offered an anti-intellectual and often anti-institutional spirituality rooted in personal piety and practical service of God and neighbor. Although Johann Arndt (1555–1621) is usually identified as its founder, Philipp Spener (1635–1705) was its classical exponent.

Spener termed the group that met at his house the *collegia pietatis,* or *pious assembly.* This group consisted of a number of laymen who gathered on Wednesdays and Sundays to pray, discuss the previous week's sermon, and study Scripture and other devotional readings, all with the goal of applying these matters to their daily lives. August Francke (1663–1727) became successor to the leadership of this largely lay movement. With Spener he advocated that people practice their devotion to Christ in service of others. Francke modeled this by opening his home as a school for poor children, founding a world-famous orphanage, and establishing a training institute for teachers, a publishing house, and a medical clinic.

The spirituality of Pietism was strongly affective and kataphatic. Holmes (1980) believes that the subjective and sentimental qualities of Pietist spirituality are its major weaknesses. Other points on which it is frequently attacked are its tendency toward legalism, its downplaying of the positive value of Christian traditions, the fanaticism it tends to spawn, and its anti-intellectual bent.

On the positive side it should be noted that Pietism was an important influence on a large number of Protestant traditions, most particularly the Moravian Brethren, Methodists, Dutch Reformed, English and American Puritans, and American Lutherans (Noll 1984, 857). Describing Pietism as a continuing force of renewal in these and other traditions, Noll notes that at its best "it points to the indispensability of Scripture of the Christian life; it encourages lay people in the work of Christian ministry; it

stimulates concern for missions; it advances religious freedom and cooperation among believers; and it encourages
individuals not to rest until finding intimate fellowship
with God himself" (1984, 858).

Puritan Spirituality

Puritanism was a loosely organized reform movement
originating in England during the sixteenth century. Its
name came from initial efforts to "purify" the Church of
England. The movement later spread to America where it
became not so much a reform movement as the attempt to
build a model society based on biblical principles.

The heart of Puritan spirituality was its focus on the
Word of God. The Puritans made a serious attempt to establish their lives on the basis of the Bible. Accompanying
this was a strong sense of accountability to God; all of life
was God's, and the quest for holiness was the central task
of life.

This God-centered view of life meant that there was no
division between the sacred and secular. The Puritans attempted to make all of life sacred and give it dignity. Spirituality was not confined to some limited sphere of activity;
spirituality was not Christian spirituality unless it encompassed the totality of life. The Puritans believed that the
true mark of Christianity was the difference it made in
how people actually live. Spirituality was, therefore, in-
tensely practical.

All of life being God's, Puritans thus expected to encounter God in the events of daily existence. In his preface to
Grace Abounding John Bunyan asked, "Have you forgot . . .
the milkhouse, the stable, the barn, and the like, where
God did visit your soul?" (Watkins 1972, 64). Or Robert
Blair, one day looking out the window and observing "the
sun brightly shining, and a cow with a full udder," wrote
that his remembering the sun was made to give light and

the cow to give milk made him realize how little he understood the purpose of his life (Watkins 1972, 30). All of life offered the Puritan opportunity for communion with God, and God was to be encountered in even the most commonplace of activities and experiences.

Another focus of Puritan spirituality was on inner experience in contrast to external appearances. Puritans often spoke of religion as a matter of the heart. They were not describing religion as an affective experience (heart vs. head) but rather as an interior experience. This led to their quest for simplicity. In worship they came to prefer extemporaneous to liturgical prayer. They also minimized ceremony and sought to cultivate a type of preaching that was practical and plainly spoken.

Leland Ryken suggests that the genius of Puritan spirituality was its ability to balance a number of crucial dimensions of the spiritual life (Ryken 1986). For example, consider their blend of the affective and speculative sides of spirituality. Puritans valued an intellectual grasp of Christian doctrine, but at the same time they valued the emotional experience with God. Similarly, they maintained a fine balance between the active and contemplative aspects of spiritual life. Puritans devoted themselves to private prayer, meditation, introspection, and Bible reading. But they were also activists. They sought nothing less than the re-formation of society.

The central images in Puritan spirituality are the warfare and the pilgrimage. Bunyan's *Pilgrim's Progress* is one of the classic writings on the spiritual life, with its depiction of the Christian life as a journey involving constant warfare. Similarly, Foxe's *Book of Martyrs* describes the Christian's warfare against the enemies of the soul: the world, the flesh, and the devil. For the Puritan the pathway to sanctification was a life of constant struggle against the powers of evil, and the Christian's task was, therefore, to prepare for this warfare by putting on the armor of God as described in Ephesians 6:10–17.

Evangelical Spirituality

Evangelicalism transcends denominational and confessional boundaries. While it is often thought of as a modern movement, its theological roots go back to the Protestant Reformation. Three principles constitute the essential theology of the movement: the complete reliability and final authority of Scripture in matters of faith and practice; the necessity for salvation based on a personal faith in Jesus Christ as Savior and Lord; and the priority and urgency of actively seeking the conversion of sinners to Christ. While these are the special emphases of evangelicalism, the movement shares many other beliefs with other orthodox Christian traditions.

The spiritual roots of evangelicalism go back much further than its theological roots. The commitment, discipline, and missionary zeal that distinguish evangelicals were features of the apostolic church, early monasticism, and the medieval reform movements. Evangelicalism's spiritual lineage, therefore, includes Irenaeus, Athanasius, Augustine, Anselm, Bernard, and a host of others who made their appearances and contributions long before the Protestant Reformation.

Evangelicals have not been known for their spirituality. Richard Lovelace in *Dynamics of Spiritual Life* writes that evangelicals have thought of spirituality as the emotional frosting on the cake of Christianity, the more substantial and important parts of which are the maintenance of sound doctrine and correct social engagement (Lovelace 1979, 12). Evangelicalism's rationalistic approach to theology and activistic approach to the Christian life have tended to often make its spirituality quite shallow.

There have been many notable exceptions. John Wesley (1703–1791) founded the Methodist movement and breathed the richness of his spiritual experience into it as well as the various Protestant traditions that have had it as their source. Eclectic in his spiritual life, Wesley read the classics of spirituality eagerly, focusing particularly on the early church fathers, William Law, Frances de Sales, Thomas á Kempis, and Fenelon. Wesley's vision of the spiritual life was that of a balance between mysticism (enjoying the love of God) and activism (developing the love of neighbor). He saw the balance between these two parts of the law as being the corrective to a righteousness of either faith or works alone.

The term *Methodism* was first applied in the 1730s to the followers of Wesley who belonged to the Holy Club at Oxford University. This was one of Wesley's Bible study classes, and the nickname *Methodist* was given to the members because of the method of their religion (personal Bible study and prayer). Their rules demanded frequent attendance at Holy Communion; regular meetings with others for Bible study, prayer, and sharing of their spiritual lives; fasting; and attendance at periodic conferences that presented in-depth teaching. Wesley also encouraged regular self-examination as a penitential discipline. The singing of and meditation upon hymns, the vast majority of which were written by John Wesley's brother Charles, also quickly became a hallmark of Methodist spirituality. In fact, a great spiritual legacy of Wesleyanism is the fifty or so hymns of Charles Wesley (out of the more than 6500 he wrote) that have become the common possession of all denominations.

But the central characteristic of Wesleyan spirituality was its emphasis on growth toward perfection. This reflected Wesley's doctrine of entire sanctification and his teachings about the steps on the road from sin to salvation. Wesley held that the process of salvation involves two crises. The first of these, conversion or justification, applies to the person experiencing freedom from sins already committed. The second crisis, entire sanctification or full salvation, accompanies liberation from the moral flaw that lies within and causes the person to sin. Such liberation provides the person with the freedom not to sin. This state, called "Christian perfection," is the goal of Wesleyan spirituality.

Jonathan Edwards's (1703–1758) life and works represent another high point of evangelical spirituality. Born the son of a Massachusetts Congregational minister, Edwards entered the ministry in the same denomination in 1726. Under his preaching his congregation at Northampton, Massachusetts, began to experience revival in 1734. As the sparks of this spiritual reawakening combined with those occurring in other New England communities, and as these sparks were fanned by the evangelistic crusades of the English preacher George Whitefield, Edwards found himself in the center of the great American religious revival of 1739–1742.

Although Edwards advanced and supported this revival through his preaching, his most significant contribution was his psychological and theological interpretation and critique of spiritual revivalism. His early writings on the spiritual revival were designed to defend it as a work of God. In responding to charges of shallow emotionalism, Edwards stressed that spiritual renewal is essentially not an emotional experience but an apprehension of the reality of God made possible by a divine gift of grace.

In *A Treatise Concerning Religious Affections* (Edwards 1959), a book that has been appropriately compared to William James's *Varieties of Religious Experience*, Edwards wrote with concern about the dangers of a religiosity that, while appearing spiritual, is actually rooted in self-love. Emotionalism, effusive religious talk, and even the experience of renewed love of God and fellow man can, according to Edwards, be self-centered and not the genuine work of the Spirit of God. True spirituality, he argued, involves both the mind and the emotions. It is not, however, the quantity of emotion that indicates the genuineness of Christian spirituality but the *origin* of such emotion in the experience with God. True spiritual revival leads to both inward changes in a person's spirit and an outflow of good works. The hallmark of God's work in the life of an individual is, according to Edwards, the replacement of self-congratulation with a hungering after righteousness and the pursuit of works of mercy and justice.

The external characteristics of contemporary evangelical spirituality are early rising for prayer and Bible study, family prayers, attendance at Sunday worship, and attendance at a mid-week church prayer service or small Bible-study group. The goal of such spiritual disciplines is personal holiness. While sometimes such spiritual discipline leads to responsible engagement with society and the world, too often it has been an exclusively individualistic matter of private piety. Lovelace argues that this failure to build bridges between interior spiritual development and external behaviors is one of the major limitations of contemporary evangelical spirituality (Lovelace 1979, 17).

Another evangelical, Donald Bloesch, sees the problem of contemporary evangelical spirituality as being its need for renewal of devotion to Jesus Christ. He writes:

> Such renewal will take the form of a deepening concern for prayer and meditation. It will also manifest itself in an awakened interest in the sacraments, particularly the Blessed Sacrament of Holy Communion. Surely a renewed devotion to Jesus Christ will also entail a passionate concern for the outcasts and unfortunates in our world, those who have been made homeless by war and famine, the victims of racial apartheid, and the diseased and forsaken. (Bloesch 1968, 15)

Bloesch compares evangelical spirituality with mystical spirituality. Evangelical spirituality, he says, is *obedience* to the will of God, in contrast to the mystic's pursuit of *union* with God. Building on this, evangelical spirituality views prayer not primarily as contemplation but as dialogue, and more specifically as supplication. Finally, and most importantly, evangelical spirituality involves a relationship with a personal God who is not so hidden in mystery that he cannot be known. He is not the impersonal "ground of our being," but is rather our Lord and Savior who has revealed himself to us in his Word (1968, 95–124).

Although Bloesch contrasts evangelical with mystical spirituality, he warns that to totally eliminate mysticism is to have a spirituality that is overly rationalistic. In fact, he later calls for the reappropriation of the mystical side of faith as a corrective to the rationalism that characterizes evangelicalism (Bloesch 1979, 281). Here he sets forth Luther's spirituality as a model for evangelicals, a model he believes preserves the hiddenness and incomprehensibility of God while affirming the fact that God can be known. True spirituality, Bloesch argues, is not a superhuman religiosity; it is simply release from bondage to sin and renewal by the Holy Spirit. In this we discover our true humanity. This emphasis on the Holy Spirit is a central feature of evangelical spirituality. Evangelicals would argue that spirituality that is not rooted in the work of the Holy Spirit is not Christian spirituality.

Another evangelical who advocates reappropriation of the best features of mystical spirituality is Richard Foster. He argues that while a number of the classical spiritual disciplines have been ignored by contemporary Protestants, they are in fact central to experiential Christianity. He sets forth concrete suggestions to aid the development of the disciplines of meditation, fasting, simplicity, solitude, confession, and spiritual guidance, along with the more commonly practiced disciplines such as prayer, Bible study, and worship.

Foster's methods are not novel; they are drawn from the history of the Christian church. For example, advocating that meditation begin with reflection upon a biblical event, he draws upon Ignatian and Salesian methods of imagination. Unlike the exegetical focus of Bible study, he states that the focus of meditation should be internalization and personalization of the message of the biblical event. He suggests that this is best accomplished by developing an imaginal representation of the event that includes as many of the senses as possible. He then suggests that this image be experienced and explored.

As you enter the story, not as a passive observer but as an active participant, remember that since Jesus lives in the Eternal Now and is not bound by time, this event in the past is a living present-tense experience for Him. Hence you can actually encounter the living Christ in the event, be addressed by his voice and be touched by his healing power. It can be more than an exercise of the imagination; it can be a genuine confrontation. Jesus Christ will actually come to you. (Foster 1978, 26)

He also encourages meditation upon creation and upon the events of the day, and suggests the utilization of breathing and movement exercises as aids to the meditative experience.

Whereas Foster presents us with a rich variety of practical strategies for spiritual development, the evangelical who has done the most work on the development of a comprehensive spiritual theology is Richard Lovelace. He says that the precondition of Christian spirituality is our awareness of our sinfulness and of God's holiness. Spiritual rebirth begins with God's forgiveness of our sins and imputation of righteousness (justification) and continues with the progressive actualization of this righteousness in our lives (sanctification). These primary benefits of salvation are accompanied by two others: the indwelling of the Holy Spirit, and our authority in Christ over the powers of darkness. The indwelling Holy Spirit makes spiritual growth possible because our spirits can now be rooted in God's Spirit, thus affording intimate and personal relationships between us and God. This clear identification of us with God means that life now, more than ever before, will involve our participation in the spiritual warfare between the forces of light and those of darkness. But in this warfare the Christian has the authority of Christ and the knowledge of Christ's ultimate defeat of Satan.

Further spiritual growth involves following Christ into the world with verbal proclamation of the gospel and social action. It also involves a deepening life of prayer, both individually and corporately. Christian spiritual life is, according to Lovelace, life in community, and spiritual growth involves increasing identification with the community of Christian believers. Within this context the final stage of spiritual growth is the progressive replacement of the mores, values, and mind-sets of contemporary culture with those of the kingdom of God, this described in the New Testament as acquiring the mind of Christ (Phil. 2:5).

Evangelical spirituality is a practical, nonmystical, predominantly kataphatic/speculative spirituality. Spiritual growth is an appropriation of the life of the indwelling Spirit of God. Evangelical spirituality is at its strongest when it emphasizes devotion to Christ and obedience to his Word, which has both social as well as personal implications. Its strength also lies in its emphasis on a direct personal relationship between the believer and God. However, its activism and rationalism have tended to make it mistrustful of deep inner experience with God, and this may be the reason for its frequent shallowness.

We began this chapter by defining the essence of Christian spirituality as experience with God made possible by the indwelling presence of the Holy Spirit. We have seen diverse ways in which Christians have defined and sought to strengthen their relationships with God. The individuals and traditions we have considered represent the entire spectrum of affective/speculative and kataphatic/apophatic possibilities. There is no single way of encountering God, and any single formula for such an experience should be rejected. God is much too big, and human personhood too complex and diverse, for our encounters with him to be simple, precisely patterned, or predictable.

But our review also requires that we add several other definitive characteristics of Christian spirituality. First, the Christian's relationship with God is not exclusively a personal possession. Christian spirituality is also corporate spirituality. The life of Christ is found in community, and growth in spirituality is similarly found in relationship with the body of Christ, the church. Do-it-yourself spirituality, so common to contemporary Christianity, is not *biblical* Christian spirituality. John Bunyan's image of the Christian's solitary walk of faith is an unhealthy view of Christian spiritual life in that it fails to represent adequately the communal nature of life in Christ.

However, the experience of deep relationship with God moves the Christian not only beyond self-encapsulation toward engagement in Christian community but also into the world. Spirituality that is oblivious to the suffering and injustice of the world is not full-orbed Christian spirituality. Christians who deeply experience God's presence in their lives do not just pray and worship, they also care for the poor and the disenfranchised and seek to correct or ameliorate social evils. The encounter with God thus situates us not only in proper relationship with God but also with others.

Christian spirituality relates to and affects all of life. Our work, our play, our sexuality, our prayers, our bodies, and our emotions are all part of our spiritual lives, comprising a relationship with God that allows us to find our true identities.

Christian spirituality involves the grounding of the human spirit in the Holy Spirit. The biblical concept of *spirituality* always implies life in and of the Spirit. Spirituality, as developed by psychologists who do not ground it in the Holy Spirit, is therefore not identical with Christian spirituality. It may be related to Christian spirituality when it regards humans as awakening to the realization that they are created as spirit and intended to transcend self in surrender to something beyond themselves. However, unless this self-transcendence is through surrender to, and life in, the Holy Spirit of God, it is not truly *Christian* spirituality.

5

Psychospirituality

Having reviewed the understanding of spirituality in a number of select psychologies (chapter 3) and in a variety of Christian traditions (chapter 4), it is now time to review and expand the definition of spirituality.

Spirituality is the response to a deep and mysterious human yearning for self-transcendence and surrender. This yearning results from having been created in such a fashion that we are incomplete when we are self-encapsulated. As important as relationships with other people are, we need something more than involvement with others; something within us yearns for surrender to the service of some person or cause bigger than ourselves. When we experience this self-transcendent surrender, we suddenly realize that we have found our place. It may be that we never before recognized that our restlessness was our search for our place. However, when we find it we immediately know that this is where we belong. Again, spirituality is our response to these longings.

In this sense all persons are created spiritual beings. To label someone as *spiritual* and someone else as *nonspiritual* is only acknowledging their differing awarenesses of and responses to these deep strivings. The spiritual person is one who listens to the messages from the innermost self and seeks to respond to them. This is what it means to say that spiritual persons are "inner directed." Their inner worlds, though unseen, are very real and of great importance to them.

However, not all spirituality is religious, and not all religious spirituality is Christian. May notes that the spiritual response becomes religious only when an individual begins to experience the self in relationship with some higher power and responds to this relationship with prayer or worship (May 1982, 33). Christian spirituality, a subset of religious spiritualities, is a state of deep relationship with God made possible through faith in Jesus Christ and the indwelling Holy Spirit. (The relationship between these various spiritualities is shown in figure 2.)

Fig. 2. **Three Kinds of Spirituality**

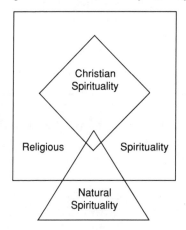

The ground of all religious spirituality is natural spirituality—the need and subsequent longing for self-transcendence and surrender, a need that is a fundamental part of our having been created in the image of God. It is quite possible to become aware of these longings and yet fail to recognize their ultimate significance, that is, the

fact that they represent the voice of God within us calling
us back to relationship with him. Persons who are aware of
these longings and who are responsive to them are doubt-
less more alive, more fully human, and better off psychologically than persons who have no such awareness.
However, from a Christian point of view such persons are
still outside the intimate relationship with God to which
their longings are intended to direct them.

Religious spirituality is a relationship with the power or
being who serves as the focus of self-transcendence and as
the meaning of life. This may be a movement toward the
true God or it may be a movement toward some other god.
Such spirituality includes prayer or meditation and worship. Contrary to their claims, much of what occurs within
groups such as Alcoholics Anonymous does not merely
support a natural spirituality, but it also nurtures a religious spirituality. Those seeking help are encouraged to
turn over control of their lives to a higher power and then
to develop a relationship with this power through meditation and prayer. While it is possible to encourage a
nonreligious spirituality, May notes that "no spiritual
quest can progress very far without becoming religious"
(1982, 33).

In Christian spirituality the probings and responses to
deep spiritual longings are carried out within the context
of the Christian faith and community. The Christian who
is growing spiritually lives in the Spirit of God with an ever
deeper awareness of being in the presence of God. The integration of personality and direction to life that flows from
this are discovered in the light of God's presence.

There are many forms which Christian spirituality takes. The spiritual pilgrimage of each person is an
individualized response to the deep inner call for self-
transcendent surrender and service. Prescribed spirituality is not really Christian spirituality but authoritarian
religion. Spirituality can be guided, nourished, and supported, but it cannot be externally manufactured or controlled, and the attempt to do so produces a sham

spirituality that does not grow from out of the heart. It can also destroy a more genuine spirituality that may have been developing.

Christian spirituality begins in and grows out of a life of interiority. True, the reference point for the self is not itself but God, who is outside and beyond the self. However, God meets us within the depths of our selves, and it is here that we relate to God and are changed by this relationship. This is the difference between spiritual transformation and religious transformation. Spiritual growth starts from within, in the heart, and spreads outward. Religious changes are exterior and much more superficial. Unfortunately, they are also more common. They comprise mere behavioral compliance with exterior standards. Not that spiritual transformation of the Christian is unrelated to exterior reference points. God's will for us as revealed in Scripture is the supreme reference point for our spiritual growth. However, the external transformation that is empowered and directed by a change within—a new spirit— is what God desires. More important to the relationship with God than changed behavior is the changed heart.

Genuine Christian spirituality is like a delicate flower. We must care for it with extreme sensitivity, ever guarding that we do not allow others to trample it. It must be watered and fed; but its growth cannot be rushed nor manipulated. The direction our spiritual development takes must remain outside the control of others as well as ourselves. We will, therefore, from time to time experience anxiety about where these developments are taking us. But the Christian need not fear, because the spirit within is not some unknown or alien spirit but the Holy Spirit, the Spirit of Jesus whom we know (John 14:16–17).

With this understanding of Christian spirituality, let us now return to the unanswered questions of earlier chapters: What are spiritual problems and how do they relate to psychological ones? More basically, what is the relationship between the spiritual and psychological aspects of persons?

The Unity of Personality

Succinctly stated, the model of personality that best fits both the biblical/theological data and the psychological data is that of a psychospiritual unity. We do not have only a part of personality that relates to God or yearns to be in such a relationship. The totality of our being yearns for and responds to God.

Furthermore, our relationships with God are mediated by the same psychological processes and mechanisms as those that mediate relationships with other people. The spiritual quest is, at one level, a psychological quest, and every psychological quest in some way reflects the basic spiritual quest. Furthermore, psychological and spiritual aspects of human functioning are inextricably connected, and any segregation of spirituality and psychology is, therefore, both artificial and destructive.

Theological Foundations

Until recently there has not been a consensus among theologians as to the picture of personality presented in Scripture. Discussions of the biblical view of persons have usually taken the form of arguments over the number of basic parts a person has, dichotomists arguing for two (body and soul) and trichotomists arguing for three (body, soul, and spirit). But increasingly the suggestion is being made in theological circles that to ask how many parts a person has is to ask the wrong question of Scripture.

The Bible confronts us with more than three "parts." Even if we limit ourselves to the writings of Paul, we are forced to consider *conscience, heart, flesh, mind, old man, new man, inner man, outer man,* and many other concepts. However, to think that these terms describe disjointed persons is to seriously misunderstand biblical psychology. In his book *A Theology of the New Testament* Ladd argues that "recent scholarship has recognized that such terms as body, soul, and spirit are not different separable faculties

of man but different ways of seeing the whole person"
(Ladd 1974, 457). McDonald maintains that the biblical
discussion of persons emphasizes first and foremost their
essential unity of being (McDonald 1981, 42).

This is nowhere more clear than in the Old Testament.
The very possibility of breaking a person down into component parts was completely unthinkable to the Hebrew
mind-set, which was not concerned with details but with
the totality. This means that to read into the Hebrew description of persons an analysis of parts is to seriously
misunderstand both the intent and psychology of the Old
Testament writers. The basis of Old Testament psychology
is that persons *in their totality* stand in relation to God and
can only be understood in the light of this relationship.

Witlock expands this idea in a paper entitled "The
Structure of Personality in Hebrew Psychology." He asserts that a fundamental Hebrew belief was the essential
and irreducible unity of personality. Parts are understandable only in the context of the whole.

> It is not the body nor the mind which acts but it is the total
> person. It is the total "I" who confronts God. It is the total
> "I" which is responsible to God. . . . To the Hebrew, evil re-
> sides in the total person. It is the whole man who sins. . . . In
> the Hebrew concept of repentance the person repents not
> for the separate acts which he has committed, but for being
> the kind of person (the totality of his person) in which sinful
> acts could originate and be committed. (Witlock 1960,
> 10–11).

Hebrew psychology was, therefore, clearly a wholistic
psychology. Parts were never seen as ultimate realities but
only as conceptualizations having no independent existence. They were seen as different aspects of one vital and
integral personality.

When we turn to the New Testament we encounter a
broad range of anthropological concepts that, again, indicate not parts or components of persons but characteristics of whole persons. Berkhouwer summarizes it as

follows: "No part of man is emphasized as independent of other parts; not because the various parts are unimportant but because the Word of God is concerned precisely with the whole man in relation to God" (Berkhouwer 1962, 200). He goes on: "It appears clearly, then, that Scripture never pictures man as a dualistic or pluralistic being, but that in all its varied expressions, the whole man comes to the fore" (1962, 203).

In summary, it is clear that the scriptural view of persons is a wholistic one. The basic teaching on human personality presented in both Old and New Testaments is that of the unity of our being. "Human individuality is of one piece, it is not composed of separate or independent parts. This assertion is essential to the theology of the whole Bible" (Laidlaw 1895, 55).

Humans are not a composite of a number of parts; we do not "have a spirit" or "have a body"; we are embodied spirits. Thus, while it is appropriate to speak of attributes or characteristics of personhood, these must always be understood in the light of the basic wholeness of personality. Leech states the matter as follows: "The Christian gospel is concerned with the human person, with his loves and his fears. So there can be no easy division of that person into 'spiritual' and 'psychological' any more than we can divide him into 'body' and 'soul.' It is the whole person that breathes, experiences, and worships God" (Leech 1977, 106).

Humans are ultimately only understandable in the light of this primary and irreducible wholeness. It makes no sense, therefore, to break persons apart in order to attempt to understand them. This should not only serve as a critique of reductionistic methods of psychology, but it should also indicate the absurdity of attempting differential diagnosis of psychological and spiritual problems. Soul *(psychē)* and spirit *(pneuma),* concepts used interchangeably in Scripture, present us with two perspectives on the inner nature of persons. "Spirit denotes life as having its origin in God; and soul denotes life as constituted in man" (McDonald 1981, 79). Both, however, describe the immaterial inner core of human personality, our psychospirituality.

DeGraaff adds an interesting footnote to these conclusions by noting that the impetus to the current theological emphasis on the unity of personhood has come not primarily from a study of Scripture but from the growing psychological consensus about the fact (DeGraaff 1977, 164). Let us, therefore, briefly consider some of these findings and conclusions.

Psychological Foundations

Not many psychologists have directly spoken of the psychospiritual unity of personality, nor can data supporting this unity be easily produced. However, two areas of psychological research, psychosomatic disorders and biofeedback, both speak indirectly to this matter. By demonstrating the close interconnection between mind and body, and thereby attesting to the basic unity of personhood, research in these areas indirectly supports the thesis of the psychospiritual unity of personality.

Psychosomatic disorders are physiological dysfunctions that result primarily from psychological processes, rather than from immediate physical pathologies. A decade ago it was common to think of these disorders as representing only a small percentage of all health disorders. However, current estimates range from 30 percent to as high as 90 percent, with an emerging consensus being that a majority of illnesses have both psychological and physical causes (Bakal 1979, 9). This suggests that the label *psychosomatic* is misleading and perhaps should be abandoned. In its place we need language that helps us remember that most, if not all, disorders represent some interaction of psychological and physical processes.

Another area where we see the close interconnection of mind and body is biofeedback training. The fact that it is possible to change physiological processes underlying such disorders as headaches, hypertension, some forms of cardiac illness, or even epilepsy merely through presenting information to patients about what is happening in their bodies demonstrates the complex interaction that exists between mind and body and supports the argument for the fundamental unity of personhood.

It is clear that psychological variables, such as emotional states and cognitions, can change brain chemistry and subsequently produce body changes. Conversely, physiological changes in the body, such as trauma or tissue damage, can also change brain chemistry and subsequently modify emotions, thinking, and other psychological variables. Mind and body are so closely interconnected that it is no longer appropriate to view either health or illness merely as body states. It is the whole person who falls ill, not a body or some body system or organ.

With regard to the unity of spiritual and psychological aspects of personhood, no one has been more emphatic than Carl Jung. Jung's clinical experience convinced him of the deep interconnection between spiritual and psychological processes and of the crucial role spiritual considerations play in psychological healing. Consider, for example, the following:

> Among my patients in the second half of life—that is over 35 years of age—there has not been a single one whose problem has not been in the last resort that of finding a religious outlook on life. It is safe to say that every one of them fell ill because he had lost that which the living religions of all ages have given to their followers, and none of them have been really healed who did not regain this religious outlook. (Jung 1933, 164)

Although Jung's idea of spirituality differs somewhat from the one we are developing in this chapter, his witness to the essential interdependence of psychological and spiritual processes is clear.

My own research and clinical experience also support the argument for the deep and fundamental unity of personality. Research with patients diagnosed as having multiple personality disorders indicates that even in people with what appears to be a totally fragmented personality there exists a single unified self (Benner and Evans 1984). In such patients the fragmentation can manifest itself in the presence of up to several hundred different alter personalities, each with unique self-concepts and self-presentations, values, moods, aesthetic tastes, sexual orientations, and patterns of physiological response. However, underlying the obvious and very real differences is a coordinated self-system that makes it possible to discern a unity of selfhood. Treatment is seriously hampered when the therapist accepts the veracity of the patient's experience of self, that is, of a number of persons inhabiting a single body. Only by helping the patient understand and experience the deeper unity of personality that exists can significant progress toward integration of personality be made.

Reviewing the movement of psychology from earlier atomistic approaches to the study of persons to the more contemporary wholistic approaches, Hall and Lindzey conclude that today nearly all psychologists subscribe to a wholistic viewpoint. They go on to state:

> Who is there in psychology today who is not a proponent of the main tenets of organismic theory that the whole is something greater than the sum of its parts, that what happens to a part happens to the whole, and that there are no separate compartments within the organism? . . . Who believes there are isolated events, insulated processes, detached functions? Very few, if any, psychologists subscribe any longer to an atomistic viewpoint. (Hall and Lindzey 1978, 270–71)

Personhood is unified in a deep and basic way. Furthermore, only by accepting this basic underlying unity is it possible to move toward greater degrees of integration of the disparate aspects of personhood. Compartmentalization creates disunity; to define some sphere of personhood as independent of and unrelated to another or to the whole is to introduce a breach into the radical unity that characterizes the human person.

Because of this fundamental unity, the spiritual and psychological reductionist positions we explored in chapter 2 provide a more accurate map of personality than that provided by the psychospiritual dualists. The reductionists' assertion that there is fundamentally only one type of problem experienced by humans in their inner lives is quite correct. However, both are naive in their understandings of the totality of personality. The problem with psychological reductionism is that it eliminates anything that falls outside naturalism and materialism, and the problem with spiritual reductionism is its overly restrictive understanding of both spirituality and psychology. Genuine Christian spirituality does include the moral concerns that characterize this reductionist position, but it also includes much more, as we shall see.

Structure and Direction

One model of the relationship between psychological and spiritual aspects of personality is the distinction Wolters makes between the structure and direction of things (Wolters 1985).* Wolters asserts that people have both a specific structure and a specific direction. The term *structure* refers to the order of creation, the individual as made in the image of God. The term *direction* refers to the fact that the individual either remains under the curse of human sin or under the blessing and progressive work of divine redemption. Therefore, persons can be seen as

---

*This distinction has its roots in the work of the Dutch philosopher Herman Dooyeweerd, who saw philosophy as the study of the structure of creation, and theology as the study of the direction of those same things.

reflecting both the original work of God in creation (structure) and either a continuing bondage to sin or a progressive restoration of their personality to the image of God (direction). Christian theology asserts that all of creation is oriented toward God, but the direction of that orientation is one of either rebellion or submissive service.

The implication of this distinction is that the psychological aspects of persons are the basic structures of their created natures, while the spiritual aspects are the directions of their personalities. And if this is the case, the inseparability of these two dimensions is clear. Even as magnitude and direction are the essential properties of a vector, so structure and direction are the defining properties of human personality. They are not equivalent. However, it only makes sense to talk about one in the context of the other, as neither has much independent meaning.

Another implication of this distinction between structure and direction is that all spiritual activities and experiences operate within the substratum of psychological structures and mechanisms and conversely, all psychological structures and mechanisms have spiritual foundation. Let us consider these implications separately.

First, the model of psychospiritual unity suggests that we relate to God through the same structures of personality as those through which we relate to other people. If we perceive God dealing with us in some way that circumvents the rational mind, it is not necessary to posit some new structure of personality as the mechanism for this. Intuition, emotions, or even unconscious mental processes are options for such a mechanism. We should not expect God to bypass normal mechanisms of functioning when relating to us. He certainly could, but why would he? There should be no threat, therefore, in the psychological study of religious experience. Explanations produced by such study do not "explain away" the experience; rather, they identify the psychological mechanisms involved in the spiritual or religious experience.

But the converse is also true. All psychological structures and mechanisms also have a spiritual basis. Even as
a shovel can be used to dig a grave or plant a tree, so, too,
the use and direction of the will, emotions, learning, imagination, creativity, or the intellect is a spiritual matter. This
does not make them spiritual mechanisms or structures.
There are no such things. The mechanisms of the spiritual
life are psychological. But psychological mechanisms inevitably have direction, and that direction comes from the
spiritual basis of psychic life.

It is clear that not all aspects of personality are directed
in the same way. When, if ever, they are, we have a thor-
oughly integrated person. All aspects of such a person's
being are centered in some integrating focus, and there is
complete consistency within that personality. This is the
ideal of Christian psychospiritual maturity, wherein all
things are in subjection to Christ. But when we fail to
reach this ideal it is not an all-or-nothing matter. Some
aspects of personality will be oriented toward God, while
others will not. However, those that are not will neverthe-
less have some other orientation.

Psychospiritual Health and Pathology

Spiritual and psychological health are intimately related. Speaking of this relationship, Howard Clinebell
states that "spiritual health is an indispensable aspect of
mental health. The two can be separated only on a theoretical basis. In live human beings, spiritual and mental
health are inextricably interwoven. What hurts or heals
one's relationship with oneself and others will tend to hurt
or heal one's relationship with God and vice versa" (Clinebell 1965, 20). This is often observed in psychotherapy,
where Christians who initially report deadness in their
spiritual lives, after making significant progress in therapy come to experience spiritual vitality (Barshinger 1977,
19). It appears that people have the same barriers and

problems in their relationships with God as they do with other people. Similarly, the same strengths and areas of health also seem to characterize both spheres of functioning. Persons capable of deep intimacy and emotional honesty in relationship with God will generally display the same strengths in their relationships with others. Let us consider these principles within the context of two case studies.

Case Study #5

Suzanne was forty-six years old when she was referred for psychotherapy by the mother superior of her convent. She had been visibly depressed for about four months, and in the past month she had stopped eating in what appeared to be a thinly veiled suicide attempt. She came for therapy quite willingly, although she was clearly very anxious about it.

In the initial sessions her history began to emerge. Suzanne was the third of three children; she had two older sisters. She reported a happy and relatively uneventful childhood, and her development up to age eleven was basically normal. At that time she was sexually molested by an uncle, whom she later realized had similarly molested both her sisters on a number of occasions. The sisters had managed to keep these incidents secret, partly out of a deep and horrifying sense of shame and partly out of fear of promised retaliation on the part of the uncle should they not do so.

Suzanne was not able to keep it a secret. Not that she wanted to tell anyone, at least consciously. However, she stopped eating, isolated herself in her room, and cried for hours on end. She finally disclosed to her parents the basis of her shame and self-loathing. As is customary in such situations, her primary reaction was not anger but shame. The anger would not surface until after many months of therapy.

Suzanne never fully recovered from this incident. She

became much more reclusive, her school performance deteriorated, and she showed a definite aversion to males. At age sixteen she made her decision to become a nun known to her family. They expressed concern about it, as they felt that it was an unhealthy retreat from the conflicts and problems resulting from the incident with her uncle. The convent supported this conclusion, encouraging Suzanne to finish school and continue to search out God's will.

She finished college and seemed to have straightened things out. Suzanne's family was aware that she did little or no dating, but when she again announced her plans to enter a convent, they expressed their support. She joined the religious order; and things seemed to go well for her for the next twenty-five years.

The precipitant for Suzanne's difficulties was an emotional attraction she began to feel for one of the other sisters. Suzanne had always managed to repress her sexual urges and had distanced herself to a considerable degree from her peers. However, over the years a relationship with one of the sisters grew, slowly at first, but then her emotional response to the woman began to quicken. This terrified Suzanne, for she also began to respond to the emotional closeness with sexual feelings. It was her conclusion that she was a homosexual that led to intense depression and self-starvation.

Over the years Suzanne had related to God in basically the same way she related to other people. She was pleasant and respectful, but emotionally distant and very cautious. In fact, she described herself as preferring to think of God as a spirit or a force, not as a personal being. The concept of a loving heavenly Father was not a part of her personal religious experience, even though it was a part of her religious vocabulary. She had created an impersonal God she could relate to, and her God was distant enough to be only a minimal threat to her fear of intimacy.

Let us now attempt to analyze and understand this woman's problems. Were they spiritual or psychological?

It is quite apparent that they were both. In fact, one core psychospiritual problem that impaired Suzanne's functioning was her fear of intimacy. This led to her avoiding people, emotions, and experience of any kind as much as possible. She was afraid of life, of really being alive. She pursued God not as part of a spiritual quest but as a way of avoiding people and the disturbing emotions such an experience would engender. She was incapable of any sort of spiritual self-transcendence, as she was afraid of experience of any sort. Self-abandonment, surrender, entering into the mystery of life, and a host of other spiritual experiences were all unavailable to her, and she was thereby blocked in her growth both spiritually and psychologically.

As the roots of her fear of intimacy were resolved through therapy, and as she came to understand the life-long patterns that had become associated with it, Suzanne experienced new freedom and even joy in her relationships with people. She started to develop relationships with several of the sisters and did not avoid that special friendship that had previously been so frightening for her. She also became able for the first time to actually experience God, not to merely use some idea of him as an escape from life. She described herself as relating to God, learning to love him and experience his love for her, concepts she had previously neither understood nor experienced.

Suzanne's problems fell into both sides of the structure/direction distinction discussed earlier. Her limited capacity for trust and intimacy were structural problems. The fabric of her personality was damaged by a trauma in her childhood, and failure to mend this breach had resulted in the tear widening and the whole fabric being weakened. This was the psychological aspect of her problem.

But personality is alive. Unlike a rock that can "just be" and need not have direction, personality always has direction. The direction of Suzanne's personality had appeared to be toward God, but in fact she for the most part turned in toward herself. In spite of her religiosity, she was not alive spiritually. Her spirit had been buried many years earlier, and she preferred it to remain that way. In fact, the stirrings in her emotions, which led to her getting help, reflected a deeper stirring in her spirit as she began to allow herself to experience human love for the first time in many years.

The outcome of her therapy was that Suzanne headed in a new direction. For the first time since age eleven she stopped running from her past. She was now able to look beyond herself, and the result was spiritual growth through her new pattern of relating to others and to God.

Suzanne's religious vocation and her overt spirituality could conceivably stand in the way of making a generalization based on her case, so we will next look at the case of a person in very different circumstances.

Case Study #6

Allan had completed all but his dissertation for a Ph.D. in English literature when to the surprise of everyone he dropped out of his program and became a sailing instructor at a yacht club. He told his friends that this was a temporary job while he planned what to do next. He worked for eighteen months and then took a job as a bartender. Although he told his friends this would be another short stint, six years later he was still employed at the same bar. Liked by almost everyone who met him, he was witty, artistic, and clearly intelligent. Adept in any social situation, he exuded confidence and put people at ease.

Yet Allan seemed to be wasting his life. Friends who joked about the first year after the Ph.D. program being a sabbatical began to be concerned as year after year passed and Allan was going nowhere. He was unhappy with his situation as well. He was increasingly restless and yet was unable to follow through on any of his plans to get on with his life. Gradually his abuse of alcohol increased, until the owner of the bar warned him that if he caught him drinking on the job one more time he would be fired. His use of drugs was also increasing. Allan defined it as recreational drug use, but the pattern of dependence was becoming clear even to him.

When Allan came for therapy he stated that he wanted help to overcome his drug and alcohol abuse. However, after a short time he saw that the chemical dependence was but a symptom of more serious underlying problems. For the first time he became aware of just how angry he was at his parents and how afraid he was to grow up and take responsibility for his own life.

Allan's parents were both highly successful professionals. His mother was a concert violinist and his father was a professor at a major university. Allan was their only child. He had grown up with the privileges and pressures of life in an upper-middle-class home. In therapy he came to recognize that dropping out of his Ph.D. program was an indirect expression of his resentment toward his parents for the pressure they had placed on him to achieve. He also came to understand how his accommodation to their expectations until that time had helped him avoid the anxiety he now experienced over taking charge of his own life. He had been frozen in this anxiety for the past six years, and his drug and alcohol abuse were escapes from this painful emotion. They were also ways of dealing with his anger, which was disruptive to him but which he still had a hard time acknowledging.

At no time during Allan's therapy was the concept of spirituality discussed. However, the issues with which he was dealing demonstrated the same psychospiritual character as those in Suzanne's case. On the structural side Allan was dealing with repressed anger and anxiety associated with his fear of not pleasing his parents and of taking responsibility for his own life. On the directional side he was directed toward himself and not yet aware that this meant having his back turned on God. But this posture was dissatisfying. His chemical dependency reflected his need for a truly fulfilling dependent relationship, that of spirit grounded in the Spirit.

The only point at which Allan's spirit came alive and entered at all into the human spiritual quest was in reading. He loved good literature and could rise above himself whenever he read. However, his ambivalence over fulfilling his parents' expectations for him had led to his avoiding the kinds of books he associated with his doctoral studies, so he had in the past few years shut out even this avenue of spiritual awakening. He continued to feel some stirrings calling him toward life, but his fear led to his choosing the pseudo-experience of drugs and alcohol. These also served to deaden the spiritual stirrings which would have otherwise been disruptive.

Another way in which Allan was blocked from spiritual life was his fear of solitude. He was addicted not primarily to chemicals but to stimulation, to distractions. He avoided being alone with himself at all cost. To be still was to run the risk of hearing the stirrings and messages from his inner self and it was from these that he was running.

Allan's therapy resulted in his being much more comfortable with himself and opened the possibility for spiritual development. Knowing and accepting himself, he was ready to move beyond self. He saw that the place he had made for himself did not satisfy his deepest longings, and as a result he returned to school to attain his Ph.D. This was a step not only toward a career but also toward a spiritual place of identity. The degree would not be what he ultimately sought. However, beginning to respond to his inner wishes and longings put Allan in touch with his spiritual questing. He had not yet become aware of his need to serve something or someone bigger than himself, but his psychological growth made possible his awareness of spiritual longings and subsequent spiritual growth. This spiritual growth would be neither automatic nor inevitable. As Allan had once creatively escaped the stirrings of his spirit, so he could now find a substitute for genuine spiritual growth if he so chose. But he also now had the opportunity to hear the call of his spiritual longings and genuine spiritual growth was possible.

Psychospiritual Growth

The analysis of these two cases suggests that psychological growth (structural development) may have to precede spiritual growth (direction). While our intuition tells us that the structure of personality has to reach a certain level of development before its direction is meaningful, we should consider this matter more carefully in order to ensure that our metaphors are not misleading us.

Maslow says that lower level needs take precedence over higher level ones until the lower level ones are being met consistently (Maslow 1970). Thus, the individual who is constantly worried about where the next meal will come from is not likely to experience needs for self-actualization or aesthetic gratification. Similarly, until one *has* a self it is difficult to *transcend* self. The psychotic individual has a hard time hearing the spiritual call, or distinguishing it from the other messages arising from within, for selfhood has never been securely achieved.

But in addition to the basic development of a sense of self, true self must be discovered and differentiated from the false self a person generates as a defense against the anxiety of being a true self. In contrast to psychotics, neurotics are in a better position to separate out external from internal stimuli. But in that they are preoccupied with defending a false self they, too, have trouble transcending self.

In all of us the unfinished business of the self keeps asserting itself until it is resolved. When it is resolved we can better become aware of deeper needs and strivings. After self is securely established it must be distanced from the false self. False selves can only be *defended;* only true selves can be *transcended.* And in this self-transcendence, true self is ultimately discovered.

This does not mean that all psychological needs must be met or all psychological conflicts resolved before people are capable of responding spiritually. We can begin to respond spiritually as soon as we are capable of hearing a call to deeper spiritual realities. However, psychological conflicts and problems may limit how far we can go in responding to this call, and certainly they impair our hearing of it.

Also, this does not mean that spiritual growth automatically follows psychological growth. It is undoubtedly quite common for psychotherapy, as it is usually practiced, to lead to psychological growth and not be followed by spiritual growth. What results in this situation is a person who may rest satisfied with self-understanding, self-acceptance, or even self-actualization and fail to see that these should not be goals in themselves but way stations to and by-products of self-transcendence and spiritual surrender.

The way in which unfinished psychological business blocks spiritual growth is that it keeps us self-bound. Psychopathology deadens spiritual sensitivity and impairs spiritual response by means of the self-preoccupation that results from it. This narcissistic self-encapsulation is the essence of both sin and psychopathology (Sugerman 1976). It is not sufficient to say that we should merely die to self or give up self. Self must be known before it can be given up; we cannot turn over to God things about ourselves of which we know nothing. In spite of self-preoccupation, most people do not truly know themselves. Their focus has been not their true selves but their hurts and anxieties and their false selves, the selves they think themselves to be. They cannot give them up until they see them as false selves. In other words, they cannot transcend self until they move past the various false selves that are their preoccupations and block them from real life. Then, coming to see their true selves they are able to understand their need for surrender to God.

This distinction between the true self and various false selves that form a neurotic encrustment around the spirit may be helpful in dispelling an erroneous myth about the different paths toward wholeness suggested by psychotherapy and Christianity. The myth suggests that while

Christian spirituality means a denial and crucifixion of self, psychotherapy brings an actualization and strengthening of self.

At its best psychotherapy involves the crucifixion of the false self, which is comprised of the ways in which we protect ourselves from encounter with the deepest aspects of our being. Associated with this false-self system is a self-concept that we struggle to defend, regardless of what life may reveal to us about ourselves. This false self blocks us from growth and must be seen for what it is, a defense against the deeper experience of our true self and of life. Psychotherapy brings us to this insight. At this point we know ourselves as we truly are and understand the reality of our existential condition. We are then able to respond to the inner spiritual call, to crucify self-centeredness, and to look to God rather than self as the Lord of our lives. Crucifying the idolatrous self-as-god, we are then free to know ourselves as we never could before; we can now know and actualize our self-in-God.

Discussing this process, Barshinger states that "self-denial requires a great deal of self-focus. It is necessary to know yourself to know God more deeply" (Barshinger 1979, 10). The focus on the self is not the core of the non-spiritual person's problem. The core problem is making the self god. It is this idolatrous posture which we must crucify.

But is it ever the case that a response to the spiritual call is the catalyst for psychological growth rather than the other way around? This certainly seems to be true, but psychologists probably know less about such people merely because they are less likely to come to their attention. Popular Christian literature is full of accounts of people whose lives are transformed by spiritual rebirth or a new and deeper experience of Christ in their lives. And occasional reports of such do appear in the professional psychological literature, reinforcing the popular reports with more systematic and rigorous investigation and followup (see Pattison and Pattison 1980).

The norm (in people possessing the necessary psychological maturity) is that spiritual growth should lead to psychological growth. People who appear to be spiritual giants but are actually psychological cripples may not be all that they appear to be spiritually. Probably religion has replaced spirituality for them. Similarly, people who appear to be well adjusted and healthy psychologically but who are not participating in the human spiritual quest are not as healthy as they appear. To be spiritually dead, that is, to be unresponsive to the deep call from within to find one's place in submission to God, is to be psychologically underdeveloped and impoverished.

Stages of Psychospiritual Growth

Psychospiritual maturity involves maturity of both the basic psychological (structural) aspects of personality and the spiritual (directional) aspects. Theories of human development typically focus on either the psychological or spiritual aspects but seldom on both. Such theories are numerous and often conflicting. In psychology, quite distinct developmental theories are presented by psychoanalysts, behaviorists, and followers of Piaget, Kohlberg, and others. Even within the psychoanalytic tradition, major differences in the developmental road maps exist between psychosexual theorists, psychosocial theorists, object-relations theorists, self theorists, and ego psychologists. It is therefore quite impossible to definitively establish the one true model of psychological development within the space of a few pages.

The situation in Christian spirituality is, as we have already seen, quite similar. Roman Catholics have most favored the language of spiritual development and have proposed a number of models, all rather closely related to the three steps of purgation, illumination, and union with God. During the Reformation, Luther condemned Catholic developmental language, but within a century Lutheran Pietists were formulating models for the stages in spiritual growth. Calvin reordered and redefined the three classic Catholic stages of spiritual growth as justification, sanctification, and glorification. Some of the most detailed Protestant alternatives to traditional Catholic models of spiritual growth were the products of Puritan theologians.

I will not attempt to review any of those models of psychological or spiritual development. To do so would take us too far from our primary goal of understanding the relationship between psychological and spiritual aspects of persons. What I will do is sketch the contours of my own model, which includes both structural (psychological) and directional (spiritual) milestones of psychospiritual development. The section on structural development in this model is based on Heinz Werner's orthogenetic theory which suggests that the essence of development is the movement from fusion toward differentiation and subsequent integration (Werner 1961). The section on directional development summarizes evangelical thought on the subject. The essential parts of my model are summarized in figure 3.

Fig. 3. Stages of Psychospiritual Development

Structural Milestones	Directional Milestones
1. Symbiotic dependency	1. Development of basic trust
2. Differentiation of self	2. Awareness of call to self-transcendence
3. Relatedness	3. Recognition of call as from God
4. Individuation	4. Awareness of insufficiency of self (sinfulness)
5. Self-transcendence	5. Receipt of divine forgiveness
6. Integration of personality	6. Progressive freedom from sin
	7. Progressive evidence of the fruit of the Spirit
	8. Deepening intimacy with God

We will first consider the structural and directional milestones separately. Then we will examine the ways in which they interact.

Structural Milestones

Although they might describe these stages differently, most developmental psychologists recognize psycho-

logical development as being the movement from an un-
differentiated psychological fusion with the mother
toward a differentiation of self and a subsequent integration of the various aspects of self into a stable personality.
They differ with each other as to what, if any, the additional stages are in this process. My model has three additional stages subsequent to the differentiation of self from
the mother, this normally occurring somewhere between
eighteen and twenty-four months of age, and before the
complete integration of personality. The additional stages
are relatedness, individuation, and self-transcendence.

Once the infant realizes the reality of his or her separate
identity from mother, the next major developmental task
is learning to relate and attach to others in nonsymbiotic
ways. These attachments operate within the recognition of
the separateness of self from others; that is, ego boundaries are preserved. This is the fundamental difference between the infantile (or psychotic) attachments, which are
present in adults who fail to recognize ego boundaries,
and the more mature attachments of adulthood. The
boundaries between self and others must be clear to us,
but we must then find ways to bridge them. Reaching out,
we must learn how to establish contact and meaningful
engagement with other people.

The quest for identity is sometimes incorrectly defined
as an introspective retreat from others, a kind of examination of one's psychic navel. However, to attempt to find self
apart from others is to fail to find our true selves. True selfhood is a gift we receive from others; in relationship to
others we find who we truly are. Developing meaningful
attachments to others is, therefore, a necessary step in the
discovery of identity and the achievement of psychological
maturity. The narcissistic personality, so common in our
day, is a clear example of impoverished psychological development, self-encapsulation, and a limited capacity for
interpersonal engagement.

At the same time as we are learning to form and maintain meaningful relatedness with others, we should also be

progressing in what Jung calls individuation, that is, the formation of an alliance between the conscious and unconscious parts of self. The self that must be known for significant self-transcendence to occur is the true self. This is only discovered as we meet and accept into our conscious self-systems the shadow aspects of self that previously were hidden from consciousness. (The shadow consists of those aspects of self we do not wish to accept but that continue to control us until we acknowledge and accept their existence.) The degree of ultimate integration of the self is dependent on the extent to which we first come to know our true selves in entirety. Only then can we move beyond self in self-transcendence.

Finally, while it is possible to achieve a degree of integration of personality with only limited movement beyond self-encapsulation, psychological wholeness also requires self-transcendence. As Christ paradoxically proclaimed, to find self, we must first lose self; that is, in order to ultimately arrive at integrated whole personality we must transcend self. The importance of this surrender of self to some higher purpose or being has been little appreciated within psychology. Some humanistic and transpersonal psychologists recognize it as an important and even necessary factor in the achievement of an integrated personality (see Angyal 1958; Maslow 1970), but have usually either misinterpreted or failed to discern the ultimate spiritual significance of such surrender and self-transcendence.

The ideal is that our personalities be integrated around this self-transcendent point of reference. The pursuit of personal happiness, the achievement of financial success, or the establishment of a reputation can all be life-guiding values that can serve as points of integration for our personalities. However, these immanent points of reference fail to provide the same depth of integration provided by a transcendent point of reference. The more our points of integration lie outside of and beyond our selves, the more adequate the resulting self formation.

The process of the integration of personality can be,

and frequently is, short-circuited. It is possible to experience a stable identity and some degree of integration of personality with only minimal social relatedness and individuation and virtually no self-transcendence. However, psychological wholeness is not to be found apart from meaningful engagement with others, significant integration of conscious and unconscious aspects of personality, and a self-transcendence that involves surrender to and service of a larger cause or being.

Directional Milestones

The milestones of directional or spiritual development can be broken down into three groups. Stages 1 through 4 (see fig. 3) can be theologically described as *preparation*, stage 5 as *justification*, and stages 6, 7, and 8 as *sanctification*. The first steps of preparation are often excluded from models of spiritual development that assume that Christian spirituality begins with the new birth provided by a divine act of justification. If spiritual awareness is posited before justification, it usually comes at stage 4, awareness of sinfulness. However, it is clear that spiritual awareness and growth do not begin here but originate much earlier.

The preparatory steps begin with the infant's development of a capacity for trust and openness to life. This is the basic building block for all subsequent psychospiritual growth. Although this capacity to trust is usually thought of as a psychological milestone, I would argue that it is really a spiritual achievement. Trust is choosing to open one's self to others and to the world. Its absence is a turning of self inward upon itself. While this has obvious implications for subsequent psychological development, it is, I feel, primarily a spiritual matter in that it is related more to the direction of personality than to its structure.

Spiritual growth in the two-year-old or in the profoundly retarded or chronically psychotic adult primarily takes the form of growth in this area. Trust of, and openness to, life is a spiritual development with profound consequences for later development.

The second step is awareness of our spiritual natures as a call to self-transcendence. At this point we become conscious of strivings deep within that leave us restless. This is the longing for surrender, or a desire to find our places in the cosmos, and an awareness that this place cannot be found within human relationships, vocation, or other temporal and material things.

In the third stage we become aware that the longings we are experiencing represent a seeking of God. At this stage we may not know who this God is or by what name he should be called. Nor will we know that our longings are not merely our search for God but are also the voice of God within calling us to himself. Our awareness is, however, a spiritual awareness in that we now recognize that we seek God.

The fourth and final preparatory stage is the point where most models of spiritual growth begin. Quite conscious of the existence of God, we now become aware of his holiness and the standards of his law. According to Romans 3:20, the awareness of God's law leads to the knowledge of sin. Under the influence of the Holy Spirit, we now know our utter inability to meet God's standards. As we gaze back and forth between ourselves and God's law and righteous character, we progressively understand the depths of our sinfulness and need of a divine intervention of grace if we are to be able to approach God.

The fifth step involves this divine intervention of grace, the free pardon of sins. This is the step theologians generally refer to as justification.

Sanctification, that is, the progressive outworking of this righteousness and the restoration of our natures into the image of God, is the process of stages 6, 7, and 8. We move progressively toward greater and greater freedom from the bondage of sin. This involves spiritual warfare, for sin is not relinquished without a fight, a fight into which the forces of darkness enter as they attempt to keep us within that kingdom. However, by the power of the indwelling Holy Spirit and the authority of Christ given to the believer, we are able to move ahead through these struggles and enjoy the fruit of the Spirit described in Galatians 5 as love, joy, peace, patience, kindness, generosity, fidelity, tolerance, and self-control. Living life in the Spirit of God also makes possible a progressive deepening and mystical union with God. This intimate communion with God also furnishes the basis of the spiritual unity and communion of all believers.

Psychospirituality

This model should not be interpreted as being strictly linear. The stages in each sphere of functioning are not absolutely fixed; usually an individual is dealing with several of them at the same time. In addition, people approach God in different ways; the path of psychological growth is also variable. However, the message of this model is that growth in the two spheres is interdependent. Problems of one sphere are necessarily problems of the other. The dynamics and problems of our inner lives reflect the psychospiritual unity which characterizes human nature.

Spiritual growth requires a certain degree of psychological maturity. Both the psychotic and self-encapsulated narcissistic persons will have difficulty growing much beyond the sixth or seventh spiritual steps. Getting to these stages will certainly allow such persons the experience of the new birth, but the inability to go on will impair the capacity for self-transcendence and will limit the experience of intimate communion and union with God.

It is precisely because psychological growth is often prerequisite to spiritual growth that psychotherapy can be a springboard for spiritual as well as psychological growth. In the cases described earlier in this chapter, this is what we saw. Suzanne had made only limited movement into the third stage of psychological growth (interpersonal relatedness) and no progress in terms of the fifth (self-transcendence). Consequently, the integration of personality she had achieved was limited, and her overall psychological health modest. Therapy focused primarily on psychological growth, but had the effect of precipitating spiritual growth as well.

Allan represents someone who was functioning higher psychologically, but was even more spiritually dead. Therapy made future spiritual growth possible, as it helped him move beyond the unfinished psychological issues of his past, which until then had kept him deadened to the spiritual call. Therapy brought Allan to the second stage of spiritual development (i.e., awareness of the call to self-transcendence).

To summarize, psychospiritual maturity is characterized by integration of personality, which occurs within a context of significant interpersonal relationships and surrender to God. In this surrender we discover our true selves. The integrated self, which is the endpoint of this process, is both an achievement and a gift. In deepening intimate union with God we find the selves he gives us; we become the selves we were intended to be from eternity.

6

The Spiritual Quest

The essence of the Christian's spiritual quest is eloquently summarized in Augustine's famous prayer: "Our soul is restless until it finds rest in thee, O Lord. For thou hast made us for thyself" (Augustine 1980, 3). Created in the image of God, humans are incomplete until they find themselves in relationship to the God who created them for intimate communion with himself. This for Christians is the ultimate meaning and purpose of life.

Our creation in the image of God explains our natural religiosity.

> Man is a religious creature . . . in all of his aspects. Created in the image of God, his whole life must mirror service to his Creator. Man cannot exist outside of the service to his God. Not only must his life be religion, no, it also *is* religion. It may be that he serves the true God, the creator; it may be that he serves an idol, be it part of the rest of creation or an idolization of himself. But serve he must. Religion defines man, it is the meaning of his creation; to this end he was called forth. (Hart 1977, 77)

Others see the implication of our creation in the image of God differently. For example, McNamara associates it with our self-transcending hunger for what lies beyond our grasp (McNamara 1975, 396), and Brunner focuses on our need for social relatedness (Brunner 1939). However, underlying this variety of interpretations of the *imago Dei* is the Christian affirmation that human nature is shaped in the image of God and that this is the basis of our spiritual questing.

But it is clear that not all people do, in fact, experience a discernable or recognizable spiritual questing. Many would find Augustine's prayer to be a quaint expression of the needs of a monk that has little relevance for the modern secularized man or woman. They would assert that they feel no such pull toward God, no latent religious longings. However, a closer look at the longings and needs that such persons do experience will allow us to identify some of the ways people mask their spiritual needs. We will discern that a number of other basic human quests are, at core, expressions of more fundamental spiritual yearnings.

The Quest for Identity

It is common to think of the search for identity as an adolescent phenomenon. While it is true that for adolescents this is very much in the foreground of their experience, younger children are certainly not indifferent to it, and many adults go through much of their lives continuing to struggle with identity questions.

In the young child the search for "the real me" takes the form of "What will I be when I grow up?" Recall how fluid the sense of self was when you were six, eight, or perhaps ten years old. One day you were a future musician, while the next day you were a policeman, doctor, teacher, mommy, or astronaut. The possibilities seemed endless. But so did the quest.

In adolescence the search for identity moves from the future closer to the present. The question in this stage of life is not so much "Who will I become?" as "Who am I?" or even "Is there a real me?" The panic that often accompanies the asking of these questions is what we tend to associate with the adolescent identity crisis. However, over the course of the next few years the urgency of these questions subsides. An identity of some form is found, and late adolescents enter young adulthood caught up in jobs, careers, relationships, and sometimes marriage. These foci allow identity issues to recede from the foreground for a while. The identity question has been temporarily answered by the circumstances of life. Young adults now define identity in terms of roles: I am my job, my marital status, or my economic status.

Mid life frequently calls for a readjustment of the answers people have previously accepted. Identity once again becomes an issue. After having invested fifteen years in the children or a career, many people begin to ask if that is all there is to life. Could they, perhaps, be some quite different persons—maybe unmarried, or maybe in different careers, or maybe living in different parts of the country? These longings are really identity longings. The question is once again "Who am I? Am I to be defined by the circumstances of my life, or is there something else to me? Could I instead change my circumstances and fit them to who I feel myself really to be? Would changing the external aspects of my life perhaps be a way to discover the real me?" These questions are also spiritual questions, and the search for identity, regardless of the stage of life in which it appears, is part of the spiritual quest.

The search for identity is intimately connected with the search for purpose, which is more obviously a spiritual search. In fact, Victor Frankl believes that the quest for meaning and purpose is the primary manifestation of the spiritual quest (Frankl 1962). "Who am I?" is only satisfactorily answered when it is answered within the context of a philosophy of life. Existence then has direction, and this is ultimately necessary for stable identity. When the forty-five-year-old businessman asks if there might be any other way to live his life than as that of an identity exclusively wrapped up in his business, he is questioning the purpose of life, and in particular the purpose of *his* life. Similarly, when the adolescent asks who she is, she is also asking about the meaning and purpose of her life. The question "Who am I?" is always closely related to the more basic question "Why am I?"

The quest for identity is also a manifestation of the quest for place. "Who am I?" is another way of saying, "Where do I fit in? Where do I belong?" If we look at the patterns of restlessness in our lives, it is often possible to discern an underlying search for our place as a basic and fundamental theme. Some people change jobs every few years, others change churches, communities, spouses, or lifestyles. Others do not make such changes in their external circumstances but continue to feel out of place. Perhaps the places they have created for themselves are not where they feel they really belong, but they have no idea how to find the way home.

Such people have forgotten who they are and where they belong, and most of the time they forget that they have forgotten. But their restlessness betrays the underlying quest. They need to feel that they belong somewhere. They are searching for home. Paradise has been lost; only a faint memory of it remains. They long to return but no longer remember the way.

Another aspect of the quest for identity that demonstrates its essential spiritual nature is the quest for values. To ask "Who am I?" is to ask "What do I believe? What are, or should be, my values?" Values are personal. Our values define who we are; they come to be central planks in our identities. Only moral philosophers work with values in the abstract. The rest of us relate to values as parts of self. Or, if we are concerned about other people's values, it is because they are not our own values. But values, like purpose, clearly move us into the realm of spirituality. Value questions demand that we have an overall philosophy of life. Whether we value honesty over self-interest, and how far we go in pursuing this value, depends on how we answer questions about the nature of the ultimate good for ourselves and others.

Thus we see that one important way in which many people experience their spiritual quest is as a quest for identity and the associated quests for purpose, place, and personal values. While failing to recognize these as part of the spiritual quest, people do, nonetheless, shape their spirits by the answers and solutions they adopt. Because this identity quest has implications for the structure of personality it is also a psychological pursuit. However, its spiritual nature is clearly reflected in the manner in which identity, purpose, place, and values collectively define the direction of personality.

The Quest for Happiness

The search for happiness is riddled with paradox. Searching for happiness often results in the failure to find it. Happiness is forever elusive when its attainment is a person's primary objective. However, when other worthy things are pursued, happiness usually is a by-product.

In terms of the spiritual quest persons who continually search for happiness may be those who are closest to the underlying spiritual longing. Such persons remain sensitive to a longing for more to life, a longing that relates to their deepest spiritual needs. On the other hand, those who feel they have found happiness, who are satisfied with their lives, are likely those for whom the spiritual longings are quite dead. It is much more difficult for such persons to experience the spiritual quest.

The search for happiness is something with which we can all identify. We are sure we will recognize it when we find it and claim it as our undeniable right. We certainly know when we don't have it; at those points we feel we have been handed unfair deals by life, and we raise our clenched fists to the heavens, demanding better lots in life.

This reveals the extent to which we define happiness in terms of the circumstances of our lives. We feel sure we would be happy if our cancer were cured, if we had more money, if we had a different spouse, or if our kids would stop messing up their lives and ours.

This external focus on the source of happiness is the reason happiness is so elusive. To be cured of cancer is only to later discover a heart illness. To double our income is to still feel dissatisfied, now seeing that we underestimated how much more money we need to keep up a lifestyle. To divorce and remarry is frequently to face the same problems and dissatisfactions. This focus on externals is part of the reason some people get depressed on vacations. They spend months telling themselves they are unhappy because of their work, the cold weather, or their boss, only to discover that even on the beaches of Cancun or some other vacation paradise, happiness is still elusive.

The search for happiness is a spiritual search. It is a longing for all there is to life, for fullness of life and fullness of personhood. It is a longing born in the deep call from within to live life on a higher plane. The call is a call to self-transcendence. Happiness was never meant to be found in things. Ultimately, the call of happiness is a call to the joy of life found in intimate relationship with God.

The Quest for Success

Closely related to the search for happiness is the search for success. For many people the two are synonymous; both tend to be elusive.

Success can be, and is, defined in many different ways. Undoubtedly the most common way is to equate it with financial status. To the person who feels driven in his climb from tax bracket to tax bracket, success means to be richer, regardless of his net worth at any given point. Another person may define success as having power or visible status. At first she thinks she will be a success if she can become a partner in the firm. Then her aspirations turn to senior partner, vice president, and finally president. But now she sees her firm as being too small, and success again slips away, always dependent on increasing the visibility or size of her kingdom.

Behind our specific definitions of success often lie comparisons with someone whom we regard as successful. Note, however, that we tend to choose comparison points above rather than below ourselves. This means that we compare ourselves with those we judge to be more successful. Therefore, if we are to be successful we must be at least as successful (and usually more successful) than they. Success thus perceived is hopelessly elusive. What we likely are experiencing is competition with other persons, not a drive to meet our own personal goals or standards. Often this competition is fueled by anger or resentment, and such feelings are never assuaged by accomplishments.

Success, like happiness, is an illusory goal when equated with accomplishments or possessions. However, because of its ambiguity it serves as an excellent screen for the spiritual quest. Instead of answering the calls to self-transcendence and surrender, we define the places we seek as being external things. However, these places are much too close to where we already are; they are not the places where we will find our true identities or rest from our searching.

In and of itself the quest for success is not a bad quest. It is merely misdirected. Like all human strivings and longings, the quest for success reflects a basic desire that is good, but which has become distorted. In terms of the structure/direction distinction developed in the last chapter, we might say that structurally the quest for success is the spiritual longing to be all we can be, to be fulfilled. But when this longing is directed toward accomplishments rather than a quality of life or state of character, it is a false spiritual direction that ultimately proves unsatisfying.

The Quest for Perfection

While none of us has ever experienced anything that is absolutely perfect, pure, or right, we all seem to have some idea of the existence of these states. Our internalized image of the ideal serves as a pull toward perfection. As such, the quest for perfection is one of the greatest sources of ennoblement in human experience. However, it also rubs against the constant reminders of the imperfections of our lives and has the potential of being a source of great torment.

Psychologists usually do not see perfectionism as a virtue. At least in the people they see professionally, the perfectionists are usually tight, rigid people whose perfectionism strangles creativity and energy. Such people are driven to the obsessive pursuit of standards which, while they might be attainable by virtue of talent and opportunity, are made unattainable by rigidity. Psychologists working within a psychodynamic orientation see such people as being terrorized by harsh introjects of parents who, at least in the child's eyes, were critical, demanding, and never satisfied with their children's performances. These people usually look for professional help because of the frustration and misery produced by their unrealistic perfectionistic longings. Consequently it is easy to understand why mental health professionals regard the quest for perfection as an almost invariable symptom of neurosis.

More benign forms of perfectionism undoubtedly exist. These, in contrast, may be both adaptive and virtuous. Perfectionists are people with admirably high standards of excellence, people who are not content with sloppiness or half-hearted efforts. Their efforts must be maximal, and until the results meet their standards, such persons will continue to try to improve themselves or their performances.

Perfectionism, like idealism, suggests the faint memory

of paradise lost. Perhaps by means of an archetype of paradise residing in the collective unconscious, we somehow recall the values and possibilities of life in paradise and we long to return. Such a desire to be perfect is a good and basic aspect of our humanity. However, the road to perfection is fraught with frustration unless we operate within a framework of grace wherein we are afforded some acceptable failure that is tolerated and forgiven. Apart from such grace, our ideals are so hopelessly beyond our ability to perform that we will be forever frustrated and overwhelmed with a sense of failure.

The quest for perfection is, therefore, a spiritual quest. It is the quest for wholeness. Much more than the quest for an absence of mistakes, it is the longing for the ideal, for that which is right, beautiful, and pure. While it is easy to view such longings as naive expressions of innocence, a person who has lost all idealism and drive for perfection is a person to be pitied. Perfectionistic longings continuously remind us of our failings and limitations, but without such reminders we would more easily forget the paradise which, while lost, is the place for which we long.

The Quest for Truth and Justice

Many people in our age have become so cynical as to view the quest for truth or justice as naive. They tell us there is no ultimate truth, that truth is what we make it, whatever we believe it to be. They maintain that justice is merely a utopian concept. People assume that the preservation of self-interest is so basic to human personality that justice is unattainable apart from a total equalization of power. And this, everyone recognizes, is most improbable. But the search for truth and justice is important to a large number of people who have not yet surrendered to the message of relativity and despair.

Many who search for truth are young people who have not yet lost their idealism. Consider the passion of the university student who devours the classic writings of philosophy and religion in her search for what life is all about. Or consider the many thousands of young people in cults in America. These young men and women will do whatever their messianic leaders ask of them, regardless of how little sense it makes; they are convinced of the truth of those leaders' messages and the utopian hope of their ideals. Behind this hope and fervent pursuit of truth is the human spiritual quest.

But not only young people pursue truth. Consider the plodding, relentless investigation of the scientist who views her research not merely as a job but as a personal attempt to unravel the mysteries of the universe and thus come one step closer to truth. Or consider the psychotherapist who patiently sifts through distorted memories and misperceptions searching for the truth, truth which he knows holds the promise of setting his patient free. Or consider the psychotherapy patient. Her quest for truth may be an urgent attempt to make sense of her personal experience and penetrate the web of falsifications and confusions that have permeated her life. In whatever form it appears, the quest for truth is a spiritual longing.

Similarly, the pursuit of justice is spiritual. Consider the excitement of the student who first discovers Marx and feels hope for the correction of the social ills of which he is painfully conscious. Or consider the politician, social security administration clerk, or inner-city social worker whose motivation for daily tasks is fueled by the hope of bringing those within her sphere of responsibility the justice they deserve. Such characterizations may be described in a pejorative manner as utopian, but they are indeed utopian. The hope for justice and the belief that things should and can be better is, once again, sparked by a faint memory of paradise lost. It is part of the basic human spiritual longing.

Thus, the cry of the oppressed, also, is a spiritual cry. It is a longing for a redeemer who will save them from their plight and rule justly. We comfortable, middle-class West-

ern Christians are often puzzled by the Old Testament
psalmists who cry out for justice. Perhaps we sometimes
find ourselves shrinking from justice, fearing that we may
not fare so well under a truly just administration; our self-
interests might be jeopardized. However, the oppressed
psalmist, along with the oppressed millions of the world
today, cries out for justice, seeing his only hope to be a fair
judge who will recognize the unfairness of the present situation and bring justice. The search for justice is the
search for the kingdom of God where shalom is the result
of his just reign.

The Quest for Beauty

In the musical *Amadeus* Salieri cried out to God in distress, because he saw his passion for music not being
equaled by his abilities. Salieri's appreciation for great
music moved him to tears when he listened to Mozart perform or, even when he read the scores of Mozart's music. It
also forced him to attend every one of Mozart's concerts,
as painful as this was for him because of his rivalry with
the younger but more talented man. This passion for music was an expression of Salieri's spiritual questing in that
it both reflected his longing for and provided a limited degree of self-transcendence. Jealousy dulled and eventually
killed this spiritual flame, and he renounced God and gave
expression to his hatred of Mozart, all a result of his perception of the great discrepancy between his immense appreciation for beauty and his lesser talent.

Aesthetic appreciation is a spiritual experience. Consider the experience of being emotionally stirred by a mag-
nificent performance of some great opera or other piece of
music. Or consider the response to a great work of art. To
the person who has learned to appreciate such expressions of beauty they are as moving and possibly as deep as
any in life. Art lifts us out of and beyond ourselves.

The beauty of art can change us in some way, whether

temporarily or permanently. My son at age six saw Rembrandt's "The Night Watch" in the Rijksmuseum in Amsterdam. He stood transfixed in front of this immense painting, soaking it in. Weeks later he continued to express but one desire. After all he had seen touring Europe, he begged us to return to Amsterdam for one more day at the Rijksmuseum. Upon doing so, he went straight to "The Night Watch." Even now, years later, the experience of seeing this painting remains vivid for him.

If the appreciation of beauty created by others is a spiritual experience, how much more can it be to create such works of beauty ourselves. In *The Mind of the Maker* Dorothy Sayers says that the human act of creativity is the clearest expression of our having been made in the image of God (Sayers 1941). Human creative processes are imperfect but valid reflections of the divine Creator, and she says that as we discover and express our creativity we participate with God in creation. He created from nothing; we take what he created and gave us, and refashion it.

Maslow describes the quest for beauty as a human need, noting that aesthetic appreciation is a necessary component of self-actualization (Maslow 1970). He identifies it as one of the higher level needs; until lower level needs (such as needs for safety, sustenance, and security) are met consistently, higher level needs such as the need for aesthetic appreciation will not be experienced. However, failure to experience the appreciation of beauty is, according to Maslow, to be less than fully human.

The Quest for Stimulation

Augustine spoke of our hearts being restless until they find their rest in God. While the source of restlessness is usually unclear, the experience of restlessness is perhaps the most common component of the spiritual quest encountered by people today.

Stimulation is a readily available diversion from restlessness. Our society provides an almost endless variety of such sources of stimulation. Television, books, travel, music, sporting events, alcohol, drugs, food, gambling, consumerism, exercise, and a large number of other activities all serve as sources of stimulation and escape from restlessness. We speak of being able to relax by means of such stimulation and of being able to let go of the pressures of our busy lives. To some extent this is unquestionably true. However, we also tend to become addicted to these stimulants, or more correctly, addicted to the state of being stimulated. The escape is not simply from pressures but from our inner selves. Thus these sources of stimulation can eventually deaden our spirituality.

To grow spiritually we must be able to be still. In order to hear the quiet voices of our inner selves we must turn down the volume of the external sources of noise in our lives. We must be able to experience solitude. Henri Nouwen says that the pursuit of what he calls "solitude of heart" is the first step in spiritual growth (Nouwen 1966, 26). By this he refers not primarily to physical solitude, although he notes that we do not progress far with solitude of the heart unless we can welcome and use physical solitude, but rather to a sensitivity to our inner voices. It is precisely our desire to run from these voices that fuels our pursuit of stimulation.

While the pursuit of stimulation can be an escape from the inner spiritual call, it is important to note that seeking stimulation is not necessarily antispiritual. As with all human strivings, in the quest for stimulation we can discern an original created good which has been distorted by the fall. At its best, the quest for stimulation is a longing to be fully alive, a desire to drink fully of the experiences of life. God has made us in such a way that we are vitalized by the sensory stimulation of his creation. Life is good and is to be enjoyed to the full.

Thus the quest for stimulation can be either an expression of our spiritual longing or a diversion from it. If we run from our restlessness rather than listen to it, we will never understand its meaning or be led by it in the direction of spiritual life and growth.

The Quest for Mystery

We live in an age that attempts to eliminate mystery. Today's unexplained event is assumed to be tomorrow's discovery. We have forgotten how to stand in awe of the object or experience that transcends our understanding.

But in this world of nonmystery we find occasional experiences breaking through our defenses against awe. On a starry night we momentarily find ourselves asking questions about a universe that is expanding at the speed of light. Or, studying the workings of the brain, we continue to return to the haunting question of whether the human mind is adequately explained by electrochemical reactions in the brain. We may even begin to wonder if science actually eliminates mystery or merely covers it up with theories, which while possibly true are not complete explanations.

Rudolf Otto in his classic book *The Idea of the Holy* labels the awareness that reality transcends rational or scientific explanation as an encounter with the "numinous" (Otto 1923). Otto describes the major element of the encounter with the numinous as "creature-consciousness," that is, the awareness of our smallness when confronted by an awe-inspiring, absolute, overwhelming might of some kind. This, according to Otto, involves both fear and fascination. Much like, and related to, the experience of the young child frightened and yet fascinated by a ghost story, encounter with the numinous is encounter with the *mysterium tremendum*. Otto goes on to describe this further as follows:

> The feeling of it may at times come sweeping like a gentle tide, pervading the mind with a tranquil mood of deepest worship. It may pass over into a more set and lasting atti-

tude of the soul, continuing, as it were, thrillingly vibrant and resonant, until at last it dies away and the soul resumes its "profane," non-religious mood of everyday experience. It may burst in sudden eruption up from the depths of the soul with spasms and convulsions, or lead to the strangest excitements, to intoxicated frenzy, to transport, and to ecstasy. (1923, 8–9)

The experience of the numinous is the experience of being up against something which is wholly other, something inescapably above or beyond ourselves. The *mysterium tremendum* is a spiritual experience, and the call within it is the call to self-transcendent surrender to God.

Mystery surrounds us. We can ignore it, get angry at its continued presence, or learn to love it and allow it to lead us into a deeper experience of life. Spirituality and mystery are closely related. Mystery may not always be spiritual, but a spirituality that does not have room for mystery is shallow and impoverished.

For many people the spiritual quest masquerades as the variety of longings and experiences we have just reviewed. Seldom are these longings or needs recognized as being spiritual. Thus, when people seek help in their struggles with such needs they turn not just to clergy or religious guides but with increasing frequency to psychotherapists and counselors. This raises a number of questions. Is it legitimate or responsible for psychotherapists to see persons with spiritual struggles? If so, how do spiritual concerns fit into therapy? How does psychotherapy relate to pastoral counseling and to the re-emerging tradition of spiritual guidance? And what are the possibilities of integrating the best of these separate traditions into a truly psychospiritual therapy? It is to these and related questions that we now turn.

7

Contemporary Soul Care

Contemporary soul care is in a fragmented state of affairs. As we noted in chapter 1, while psychotherapists have become the most visible and socially acceptable physicians of the soul, paradoxically they do not usually see their work as being continuous with the tradition of religious soul care. On the other hand, those whose calling and work are within the context of Christian soul care, most notably pastoral counselors and spiritual directors, are not generally regarded by secular psychotherapists as part of the same team. Furthermore, where spiritual guidance is practiced, the relationship between pastoral counseling and spiritual guidance has itself often been unclear. Although spiritual guidance is the oldest of soul care traditions, it is probably the least familiar. Before proceeding to a discussion of the relationship among contemporary soul care options we should, therefore, briefly consider what is involved in spiritual guidance.

Broadly speaking, spiritual guidance is an interpersonal relationship designed to aid spiritual growth. Tyrrell suggests that the goals of spiritual guidance usually include growing in prayer and in the life of the Spirit, dying to sinful impediments to union with God, and experiencing his forgiveness (Tyrrell 1982, 93). Others say the real spiritual guide is the Holy Spirit and emphasize seeking discernment of his leading (Leech 1977). The role of the human guide is to assist in discerning the leading of the Spirit in the life of the one seeking spiritual guidance. Although the older term *spiritual direction* is still sometimes employed, *spiritual guidance, spiritual friendship,* or *soul friendship* are the more commonly employed contemporary terms, preferable because they avoid the authoritarian implications of the term *direction.*

Advocates of spiritual guidance argue that every Christian should have a spiritual guide. This does not mean the more general relationship of parishioner to pastor, although one's spiritual guide could very well be one's pastor. Rather, it is a more intentional, personal, and individualized relationship. Such a relationship seldom "just happens." It needs to be selected and nurtured with much care and prayer. It usually begins with a hunger for a deepening spiritual life and an awareness of the limitations of trying to walk the spiritual walk alone. Subsequent to the identification of a trusted and respected person who is judged to be spiritually mature, the next step is arriving at an agreement with this person as to the terms of the relationship (i.e., the frequency and nature of meetings, the respective roles and expectations, etc.)

Options for structuring the relationship allow considerable room for individual preferences. Edwards (1980) notes that in addition to the traditional model of one spiritually less mature person relating to another judged to be more mature, alternate arrangements include mutual guidance (wherein two people take turns serving as guide for the other) and even group guidance. Small Bible-study and fellowship groups, increasingly common in many Christian circles, may have characteristics of such group guidance. Groups formed for the purpose of Christian accountability also share some similarity. However, the most central aspect of spiritual guidance is not fellowship, study, or accountability; rather, it is discernment of the leading of the Holy Spirit and nurture in Christian growth and spirituality.

Spiritual Guidance, Pastoral Counseling, and Psychotherapy

In addition to their common ancestry in the cure of souls, spiritual guidance, pastoral counseling, and psychotherapy share several other features. All three seek to support growth of the inner person, this to be followed by behavioral changes, which should ideally flow out of and be in harmony with this inner world. They all eschew coercion and manipulation and strive for free decisions and mutual trust. However, in contrast to pastoral counseling and psychotherapy, both of which attempt the healing or alleviation of hurt or emotional distress, spiritual guidance is meant to be a way of life, not a resource for problem solving. Furthermore, while pastoral counseling and psychotherapy both give a central role to the place of understanding or insight, spiritual guidance is more oriented toward deepening a person's faith, increasing awareness of the presence of God, and furthering spiritual growth.

Gerald May illustrates this by considering possible responses to anxiety (May 1982, 129). He suggests that if you are seeking to be relieved of the anxiety you should consult a psychotherapist. If you are seeking to make that anxiety an occasion for growth and wish to understand what God is saying to you through it, you should consult a pastoral counselor. Finally, however, if your main focus is not the anxiety but rather your longing to give yourself to God more fully or to know his presence in your life more deeply, then you should seek out a spiritual guide.

While such a distinction may be somewhat helpful as a general differentiation of the basic thrust of each of the three helping relationships, it is problematic. Not all psychotherapists would agree that the goal of their work with an anxious person is alleviation of the anxiety. Existential, Gestalt, and Jungian therapists (to name but a few) would be much more interested in helping such a person understand the meaning of the anxiety, this being the first step to making it an opportunity for growth. Anxiety is sometimes best seen not as disease or pathology but as an expression of dis-ease. On such occasions it is an indication that all is not well. It is, therefore, not something that should be eliminated but something that should be understood by the patient. The underlying cause of the dis-ease should then be corrected.

Good therapeutic judgment is knowing when anxiety should be eliminated and when it should be welcomed as a message-bearer. This is not just a clinical judgment; it is also a spiritual judgment. There are obviously times when a person's anxiety is at such an intense level that it is the responsible decision to either eliminate or subdue it by psychological or chemical means. However, there are other times when psychotherapists, pastoral counselors, and spiritual guides alike should help persons with whom they work accept that anxiety and listen to the message it bears about the state of their inner worlds. These occasions present opportunities for great spiritual growth that should be welcomed by therapists, counselors, and spiritual guides.

Another problem with May's attempted differentiation of psychotherapy, pastoral counseling, and spiritual guidance is that it introduces a somewhat arbitrary and misleading distinction between psychotherapy and pastoral counseling. Most contemporary pastoral counselors believe they are providing psychotherapy. They distinguish their therapy from nonpastoral psychotherapy not so much by its techniques as by its theological basis and associated expectations. For these reasons the term *pastoral psychotherapy* is becoming increasingly popular.

But not all pastoral counselors align themselves with psychotherapy. Some operate in a manner much closer

to spiritual guidance and in distinct contrast to psychotherapy (see Adams 1970). Interestingly, this parallels
developments in "Christian counseling." Christian counselors who attempt to bring their work into conformity
with Christian beliefs and values sometimes use the adjec-
tive *Christian* to describe their counseling. While there is
considerable variety in the usage of the term *Christian
counseling*, it usually refers to either biblically based spiritual direction (Crabb 1977) or to psychotherapy provided
within a Christian view of persons and their relationship
to God (Vanderploeg 1981). In the former case such counseling aligns itself with spiritual guidance and in the latter
with psychotherapy. This suggests that there are really
two rather than three groups of soul care professionals:
psychotherapists and spiritual guides.

However, even in attempting to make a distinction between the role of psychotherapists and spiritual guides it
is important to realize that both groups deal with spiritual
and psychological aspects of persons. Discussing the arti-
ficiality of attempting to exclude psychological matters
from spiritual guidance, Leech states that "spirituality
and spiritual life are not religious departments, walled-off
areas of life. Rather the spiritual life is the life of the whole
person directed towards God" (Leech 1977, 34).

Spiritual guidance and psychotherapy both inevitably
address psychospiritual problems and aspects of person.
But as usually practiced, each could be said to have a primary focus. The primary goal of spiritual guidance is
spiritual growth, not psychological growth. If, however,
genuine spiritual growth results from the experience,
psychological growth will also usually be present or soon
follows. Similarly, the primary goal of psychotherapy is
psychological, not spiritual growth. Spiritual growth may,
however, be a by-product of psychotherapy. But if spiritual
growth is the primary aim, the person should seek out
spiritual guidance. The uniqueness of psychotherapy lies
in its primary focus on psychological growth. This focus

need not exclude spiritual concerns. However, in psychotherapy spiritual matters should be addressed in a manner different from that occurring in spiritual guidance.

Psychotherapy and Spirituality

With the exception of the rare technical intervention,
such as, for example, the behavioral treatment of a tic,
psychotherapy inevitably deals with a broad enough slice
of personality that spiritual considerations are involved.
We are always either growing spiritually, that is, becoming
more sensitive and responsive to the spiritual call in
our lives, or we are becoming more spiritually dead. At
times of crisis or transition the opportunity for spiritual
movement in one direction or another is particularly
great. This is even more so the case when we face these
times with the assistance of a psychotherapist and begin
to listen to messages from our inner selves. Psychotherapy
has, therefore, great potential as a spiritual influence. But
this potential is a two-edged sword.

There are several possible spiritual dangers in psychotherapy. The first and most obvious one is counseling with
psychotherapists who have a spiritual or religious axe to
grind. They may see religiosity as either a symptom, or
possibly a cause, of neuroses. They may, therefore, think it
is their responsibility to rid their patients of any religious
convictions. Although such therapists would probably exercise restraint out of respect for their patients' personal
values, their own personal beliefs could very well be sub-
tly communicated. The therapist's influence on the personal values of the patient in intensive psychotherapy is
immense, and in such a situation it is not uncommon to see
the patient, over time, adopting many of the therapist's
values (Parloff, Iflund, and Goldstein 1960; Rosenthal
1955).

Christians sometimes decide that the only protection against such a danger is to see a Christian psycho-

therapist. While this may indeed provide protection, and may in many cases be the preferred action, it does not have to be the only possible response to the danger. Given two psychotherapists of equal training and experience, one Christian and the other not, the choice of the Christian, if such a person has found a way to meaningfully relate the Christian faith and an understanding of psychology, is probably a good one. However, the choice of a less quali- fied or less experienced Christian over a better trained and more experienced non-Christian may be both unwise and unnecessary.

An alternative is to see the non-Christian therapist, but to also enter into a relationship of spiritual guidance with someone respected for his or her spiritual maturity. This relationship should not be an attempt to receive a parallel therapy experience, however. Therapy with two people at the same time is almost always counterproductive. But a relationship with a spiritual guide can provide a place for examining the spiritual implications of the therapy experi- ence and in turn be a spiritual watchguard.

The second spiritual hazard of psychotherapy is much more subtle. Moreover, it is a danger that the patient does not eliminate by merely seeing a therapist identified as a "Christian." This is the danger of adopting a psycho- logical spirituality and confusing it with a genuine Chris- tian spirituality. Insight, listening to the voices of the inner self, and integration of personality around the deepest as- pects of what the patient perceives to be the true self all become primary, and self-transcendence through surren- der to God is either lost or missed. Listening to dreams, understanding and being responsible to feelings, learning to discern the messages of anxieties, and cultivating inner quietness or composure are all potentially significant tools for genuine Christian spiritual growth. But when they become ends in and of themselves, and the voice of the transcendent God becomes more and more faint, psychotherapy becomes a religion, not a tool.

But psychotherapy also has great potential as a tool for

spiritual growth. If the therapist avoids defining the focus of therapy too narrowly and gives permission, either implicitly or explicitly, for the patient to raise spiritual issues and questions, the therapeutic encounter can be a place where psychospiritual matters are addressed.

One way in which the therapist can give permission for the raising of spiritual matters is, in the course of the assessment or history taking, to inquire about the patient's religious history. It is amazing how therapists who routinely inquire about developmental, medical, interpersonal, academic, and vocational aspects of their patients' histories never once ask about religious upbringing and current religious state. One has to suspect that religion has replaced sex as the great taboo subject of our age.

Therapists can open the door to spiritual considerations in therapy in an even more direct way by simply telling patients in one of the early sessions that they view spiritual issues as inseparable from psychological ones and are willing to have such concerns raised. Patients will generally respond by raising issues they judge to be spiritual in nature. Sometimes these may be explicitly religious, other times more broadly existential, and sometimes esoteric and mystical. Always, however, such an invitation enriches and broadens therapy. The value of therapists explicitly teaching patients what therapy is and how it can be best used has been empirically demonstrated (Lambert and Lambert 1984), and therapists can no longer assume that all patients know or can quickly learn what is expected of them if they are to make the best use of their therapy. The therapist who wishes to include spiritual issues as part of the therapy should, therefore, deliberately invite such considerations.

Inviting the inclusion of spiritual considerations in psychotherapy is not the same as inviting religious or theological discussion. Psychotherapy is not a good place to talk about God, prayer, scriptural interpretation, or theology. It is, however, an excellent place for people to talk about their experiences with God or the meanings of other aspects of their spiritual lives. While psychotherapy does share much common ground with other soul care professions, it is not identical to any of them. Psychotherapy approaches soul care in a unique manner. The unique way in which the psychotherapist treats spirituality is that it, along with everything else it treats, is addressed psychologically.

The person who discusses prayer with a spiritual guide should expect help in the development of personal prayer life through advice. However, if a person discusses prayer with a psychotherapist, a topic which in itself is quite appropriate, the person should expect help by gaining increased understanding of his or her experience in prayer. This is the essential contribution of psychotherapy: whatever it considers, it does so by means of exploring the meaning and experience of that topic to the person. Thus, the person's uses and abuses of prayer and the dynamics and significance of it in his or her life are all appropriate areas of psychotherapeutic exploration. However, specific suggestions as to how to pray are probably more appropriately made in a relationship of spiritual guidance.

Similarly, the topic of God should be handled in a different manner in therapy from that which is appropriate in spiritual guidance. The psychotherapist should primarily focus on the patient's experience with God. How is God understood? What are the images of God and how do they relate to the internal representations of others? How does the person relate to God? Is God seen as a harsh and punitive father, and can this be meaningfully understood in terms of his or her earthly father? Or perhaps is God benevolent but basically impotent—again, something quite clearly revealing the person's experience of his or her self and of the world. This is not to suggest that God is merely a creation of the mind. However, because persons are unified psychospiritual beings, relationships with God, self, and others are all mediated by the same internal

psychological processes. It is these processes that psychotherapists are best trained to understand. It is this,
therefore, with which psychotherapists should occupy
themselves.

A clear understanding of the unique way in which
psychotherapy addresses spirituality allows us to be able
to pronounce it a legitimate soul care service. If psychotherapy approaches soul care in a manner identical to
that of spiritual guidance, then it is an illegitimate inter-
loper on stolen territory. However, while psychotherapy is
closely related to spiritual guidance, it is unique. It is this
uniqueness that must be clear to both patients and therapists.

The therapist who views psychotherapy primarily as a
place to carry out evangelism or to make spiritual disciples has missed his or her calling. Such a person should
not be a psychotherapist but should pursue some more
overtly religious vocation. The psychotherapist should be
someone who affirms the value of alleviating human emotional suffering and of promoting growth through the re-
moval of blocks to such growth. Such a therapist would see
how this is both valid and significant as preparation for
spiritual growth. Therapeutic work has spiritual implications of immense proportion. However, to attempt to make
it what it is not, that is, a relationship primarily of spiritual guidance, is to be dishonest. The dishonesty is the act
of placing the mantle of the psychotherapist over the cloth-
ing of the spiritual guide in the hope of capturing a market
which might not otherwise be available to the religious
worker.

Recognizing the differences between psychotherapy
and other soul care approaches must also include recognizing the limitations of psychotherapy. Psychotherapy
may lead persons into a place of readiness for spiritual
growth and may even help them take significant steps
toward God. However, this is not salvation. The Christian
gospel proclaims that the mechanism of the new birth is

trust in the redemptive work of Christ, not insight or increased emotional health. Vande Kemp notes:

> While the need for ultimacy may emerge in the process of psychotherapy, . . . justification certainly is not implicit there. The journey through the depths does not guarantee salvation. While it does often have the paradoxical effect of leading the person to awareness of transcendence and ultimacy . . . it does not identify the person's ultimate need as a relationship with God nor confront the person with the need for confession or the acceptance of Christ's redemptive work. (Vande Kemp 1983, 119)

Psychospiritual Therapy

The premise of the above paragraphs is that, as usually practiced, psychotherapy and spiritual guidance are related but discrete activities. Accepting this current state of affairs, I have tried to show how psychotherapy can be maximally responsive to spiritual issues while still remaining true to itself. However, this begs the question of why psychotherapy should remain true to itself. Why should we accept the current distinction between spiritual guidance and psychotherapy? Would it not be possible for one person to play both roles? If so, what would be the contours of a therapy that sought to integrate the goals of both spiritual guidance and psychotherapy?

One important factor in the current separation of psychotherapy and spiritual guidance is that spiritual guides and psychotherapists seldom have competence in each other's spheres of specialization. A person who wishes to integrate psychotherapy and spiritual guidance would have to be equally competent in the healing and growth principles of Christian spirituality and psychology. Such a person would have to be able to discern, in regard to a particular case, what combination of spiritual and psychological means should be employed at each of the various stages of the growth and healing processes. However, while it may be rare for a single person to have such competence, there is no compelling reason why it could not be developed.

One particularly exciting approach to such integrated psychospiritual therapy is Bernard Tyrrell's christo-therapy (Tyrrell 1982). At the center of this approach is Tyrrell's assertion that Christ is directly and intrins-ically related to the healing not only of sin, but also of psychopathology. Tyrrell argues that Christ, not any thera-pist, is the healer, and his healing is intended for the whole person. Tyrrell goes on to assert that, while christotherapy is particularly appropriate for a Christian who wishes to pursue growth and healing in an explicitly Christ-centered context, it is important for the person to realize that whether or not he recognizes Christ's presence, Christ is in fact present in all healing and growth. "Christ, through his Holy Spirit, is at work at least 'anonymously' in the healing and growth of all individuals who are anywhere struggling with sin, neuroses, or addictions and with the summons to move toward higher levels of wholeness and holiness" (Tyrrell 1982, 5). Christotherapy actively ac-knowledges Christ within the therapy process, appropriat-ing the healing that is made possible through his life, death, and resurrection.

Drawing heavily on the approach to spiritual growth set forth in Ignatius's *Spiritual Exercises*, Tyrrell's model of psychospiritual therapy integrates the principles of healing and growth present in Christian revelation, the Ignatian *Exercises*, and secular psychotherapy. Chris-totherapy's overall framework is drawn from the basic goals of each of the four stages or "weeks" of the Ignatian *Exercises*. This is the classic formulation of the goals of the four weeks of the *Spiritual Exercises*.

First week: to reform the deformed

Second week: to conform the reformed

Third week: to confirm the conformed

Fourth week: to transform the confirmed

Tyrrell makes creative use of this formulation, identifying the four basic functions of christotherapy as *reforming, conforming, confirming,* and *transforming.*

In the *Exercises* the goal of the first week is reformation. This is an unmasking of personal deformation (sin), and an awareness of the need for the redemptive grace of Christ. In christotherapy reformation is this same process of repentance for sin. An awareness of who we are before God, and the awful reality of our rebellion against him, is the beginning point of all true psychospiritual growth.

Conforming is the active turning toward Christ, which must follow turning away from sin. Here the goal is conforming the self to the mind of Christ (Rom. 8:29), bringing about a new disposition of heart and mind that will allow a person to grow and deepen in love of God.

Confirmation is the affirmation of our death to sin and our lives as new creations in Christ. We confirm our initial turning from sin through the sure knowledge that we are baptized in Christ's death and thereby raised to life in him (Rom. 6:3–4). Love for Christ deepens as the Christian seeks to be one with him in his suffering and his self-sacrificing service to others.

Transformation is the movement from identification with Christ in his death to contemplation of him in his glorification. Rejoicing with and for Christ because he is now in glory, we are freshly empowered by the Holy Spirit to turn more fully toward Christ and thereby be transformed into his image (2 Cor. 3:18).

Within this overall framework of spiritual growth, Tyrrell suggests that the basic methods of the christotherapist are existential loving, existential diagnosis, existential appreciation, existential clarification, mind fasting, and spirit feasting. Let us briefly examine each of these in turn.

162   **Psychotherapy and the Spiritual Quest**

Existential loving means "taking delight in the uniqueness, inner value and worth of another person" (Tyrrell
1982, 117). Such love for a person is a re-enactment of the
primal affirmation that took place at creation, the affirmation that persons are good and of immense value. The
christotherapist wants to see this value of others just as
they are seen by God. To see another person in this light is
to see past neuroses and sin, which distort and disfigure,
to the inner person.

Existential loving is not, however, a loving of some dis-
embodied spirit. It is loving the whole person, a loving
made possible by seeing beyond the surface. It is also a loving that goes beyond a mere desire for the good of the
other. It necessarily involves liking, and Tyrrell argues that
the therapist should refer the patient he or she does not
like to someone else. Existential loving is the necessary, although insufficient base upon which all the other methods
of christotherapy hang. Not liking the other person makes
providing effective help impossible.

Existential diagnosis is the identification of the existential meaning of whatever spiritual, psychological, so-
matic, or external difficulties are troubling the one
seeking help. In this process the christotherapist seeks
insight into the beliefs, values, and assumptions that are
central to the person's life and that generate either psychospiritual and physical wholeness or illness. Tyrrell believes that an individual is in existential error when, either
consciously or unconsciously, he or she "is living according to false beliefs about what true fulfillment is and how
it is to be realized" (Tyrrell 1982, 120). Existential diagnosis, therefore, is aimed at the Spirit-guided identification of these basic errors in life orientation.

Existential appreciation is the identification and re-
inforcement of those qualities of the person that enhance
and enrich life. This is an important corrective to the tendency in therapy to focus only on problems and pathology.
The christotherapist tries to see the person behind the
problems. Appreciation, like discernment, implies pene-

trating the surface, but what it uncovers is that which is of value in the individual.

Tyrrell suggests that these twin activities of existential diagnosis and appreciation are at the very heart of christo-therapy. They are both acts of discernment that require the therapist to be deeply dependent on the guidance of the Holy Spirit. They also require that the therapist be a person who knows him or her self. Such discernment must first be applied to one's own self before it can be use-fully offered to anyone else.

The method of existential clarification is the process by which the christotherapist communicates his or her diag-nostic and appreciative discernment to the one seeking help. The goal is to replace erroneous ways of approaching life with truthful ones, and to enhance those qualities of the person's life that already reflect truth and righteous-ness. This stage of therapy typically involves a broad range of methods including mutual prayer, guided meditation, confrontation, and encouragement. However, Tyrrell points out that while the christotherapist can clarify and create optimal conditions for the occurrence of existential understanding, the accomplishment of this understand-ing cannot be produced by techniques. It is a gift of God that cannot be effected by either the therapist or the one seeking help.

The techniques of mind fasting and spirit feasting are meditative disciplines that are to be practiced by both the therapist and the one seeking help. They are used through-out the various stages of christotherapy and are intended to become lifelong daily habits. Mind fasting means to focus on some problem or negative experience and then to pray for diagnostic discernment. The person then finds the meaning of this negative factor in his or her experience and becomes aware of and committed to those actions con-sistent with this insight. Spirit feasting is the same process applied to positive data, with the prayer being for an ap-preciative discernment of the experience. Taken together, these two techniques form the backbone of therapy as the person seeking help learns how to discern truth from error and then how to live that truth.

Tyrrell's reason for developing christotherapy was his conviction that it is not necessary that psychotherapy and spiritual guidance be so distant from each other. The above outline suggests one way in which they can be integrated. But it is not the only way. Other approaches to psychotherapy and spiritual growth could be integrated to produce countless other models of psychospiritual therapy. The beginning point is the conviction that spirituality and psychology belong together. Once we are sure of this, the possible ways of creatively enhancing the psychological and spiritual growth of people are endless.

If Christian psychotherapists and spiritual guides could learn to respect each other and work more closely together, the result would be a great enhancement of the healing and growth that each group is able to provide. Both groups are in unique positions to help certain people. Clergy and other spiritual guides can help those who already see their struggles in spiritual terms. But in order to provide the greatest help they must come to see spirituality as being ultimately grounded in a person's psychosomatic existence. Spirit is inextricably connected to psyche and body.

Psychotherapists may be in the best position to help those who view their struggles in psychological terms. For many non-Christians, no one else will ever get as close to spiritual issues in their lives. The psychotherapist who is sensitive to the fact that the interior world is not neatly divided into psychological and spiritual compartments is, therefore, a person who may have the unique opportunity to provide help, not merely for the structural aspects of personality, but also for the questions of life's direction. For Christians, such a psychotherapist can often make the difference between living as psychospiritual cripples and coming to experience the abundance of life that is ours in Christ.

References

Adams, J. 1970. *Competent to counsel*. Grand Rapids: Baker.

Angyal, A. 1958. *Foundations for a science of personality*. Cambridge: Harvard University Press.

Augustine. 1980. *Basic writings of Saint Augustine*. Ed. and trans. W. Oates. Vol. 1. Grand Rapids: Baker.

Bakal, D. 1979. *Psychology and medicine: Psychobiological dimensions of health and illness*. New York: Springer.

Baldwin, J., ed. 1957. Psychotherapeutics or psychotherapy. In *Dictionary of philosophy and psychology*, vol. 2, 394. Gloucester: Peter Smith.

Barnhouse, R. 1975. The spiritual exercises and psychoanalytic therapy. *The Way Supplement* 24 (Spring): 74–82.

Barshinger, C. 1977. Intimacy and spiritual growth. *The Bulletin of the Christian Association for Psychological Studies* 3: 19–21.

———. 1979. Congruent spirituality. *The Bulletin of the Christian Association for Psychological Studies* 5: 10–13.

Benner, D. G. 1983. The incarnation as a metaphor for psychotherapy. *The Journal of Psychology and Theology* 11: 287–94.

Benner, D., and S. Evans. 1984. Unity and multiplicity in hypnosis, commissurotomy, and multiple personality. *The Journal of Mind and Behavior* 5: 423–32.

Bergin, A. 1979. Psychotherapy. In *Encyclopedia of Psychology*, ed. H. Eysenck, W. Arnold, and R. Meili. New York: Seabury.

Berkhof, L. 1939. *Systematic theology*. Grand Rapids: Eerdmans.

Berkhouwer, G. 1962. *Man: The image of God*. Grand Rapids: Eerdmans.

Bloesch, D. 1968. *The crisis of piety*. Grand Rapids: Eerdmans.

———. 1979. *Essentials of evangelical theology*. Vol. 2. San Francisco: Harper & Row.

Bobgan, M., and D. Bobgan. 1979. *The psychological way/The spiritual way*. Minneapolis: Bethany Fellowship.

Bouyer, L. 1965. *A history of Christian spirituality*. Vol. 3. New York: Seabury.

165

Bregman, L. 1982. *The rediscovery of inner experience*. Chicago: Nelson-Hall.

————. 1985. Popular psychology, inner experience, and non-traditional religiousness. *Psychologists Interested in Religious Issues Newsletter* 10 (Spring): 1–2, 8–9.

Brunner, E. 1939. *Man in revolt*. Philadelphia: Westminster.

Buber, M. 1953. *Eclipse of God*. London: Gollancz.

Bufford, R. 1981. *The human reflex: Behavioral psychology in Christian perspective*. San Francisco: Harper & Row.

Cabot, R. C. 1908. The American type of psychotherapy. In *Psychotherapy: A course of readings in sound psychology, sound medicine and sound religion*, ed. W. B. Parker. New York: Center Publishing Co.

Clebsch, W., and C. Jaekle. 1964. *Pastoral care in historical perspective*. New York: Aronson.

Clinebell, H. 1965. *Mental health through Christian community*. Nashville: Abingdon.

Crabb, L. J., Jr. 1977. *Effective biblical counseling*. Grand Rapids: Zondervan.

DeGraaff, A. 1977. *Views of man and psychology in Christian perspective*. Toronto: Association for the Advancement of Christian Scholarship.

de Sales, F. 1950. *Introduction to the devout life*. Trans. J. Ryan. New York: Harper.

Doran, R. 1979. Jungian psychology and Christian spirituality: III. *Review for Religious* 38: 857–66.

Edwards, J. 1959. *A treatise concerning religious affections*. Ed. J. Smith. New Haven: Yale University Press.

Edwards, T. 1980. *Spiritual friend*. New York: Paulist.

Ehrenwald, J. 1966. *Psychotherapy: Myth and method*. New York: Grune & Stratton.

Ellenberger, H. 1970. *The discovery of the unconscious*. New York: Basic Books.

Entralgo, P. L. 1970. *The therapy of the word in classical antiquity*. Trans. L. J. Rather and J. M. Sharp. New Haven: Yale University Press.

Finch, J., and B. Van Dragt. 1985. Existential psychology and psychotherapy. In *Baker encyclopedia of psychology*, ed. D. G. Benner. Grand Rapids: Baker.

Foster, R. 1978. *Celebration of discipline: The path to spiritual growth*. San Francisco: Harper & Row.

Frankl, V. 1962. *Man's search for meaning: An introduction to logotherapy*. New York: Simon & Schuster.

French, R., ed. 1965. *The way of a pilgrim*. New York: Seabury.

Freud, S. 1910. Leonardo Da Vinci. In *The standard edition of the complete psychological works of Sigmund Freud*, trans. and ed. J. Strachey, vol. 11. London: Hogarth.

———. 1913. Totem and taboo. In *The standard edition of the complete psychological works of Sigmund Freud*, trans. and ed. J. Strachey, vol. 13. London: Hogarth.

———. 1926. The question of lay analysis. In *The standard edition of the complete psychological works of Sigmund Freud*, trans. and ed. J. Strachey, vol. 20. London: Hogarth.

———. 1927. The future of an illusion. In *The standard edition of the complete psychological works of Sigmund Freud*, trans. and ed. J. Strachey, vol. 21. London: Hogarth.

———. 1930. Civilization and its discontents. In *The standard edition of the complete psychological works of Sigmund Freud*, trans. and ed. J. Strachey, vol. 21. London: Hogarth.

———. 1938. Findings, ideas, problems. In *The standard edition of the complete psychological works of Sigmund Freud*, trans. and ed. J. Strachey, vol. 23. London: Hogarth.

Fromm, E. 1950. *Psychoanalysis and religion*. New Haven: Yale University Press.

Grounds, V. 1966. *Emotional problems and the gospel*. Grand Rapids: Zondervan.

Hall, C., and G. Lindzey. 1978. *Theories of personality*. 3d ed. New York: Wiley.

Hart, H. 1977. Anthropology: Some questions and comments. In *Views of man in psychology in Christian perspective: Some readings*, ed. A. De Graaff. Toronto: Association for the Advancement of Christian Scholarship.

Heisler, V. 1973. The transpersonal in Jungian theory and therapy. *Journal of Religion and Health* 12: 337–41.

Hillman, J. 1972. *The myth of analysis: Three essays in archetypal psychology*. Evanston: Northwestern University Press.

Holifield, E. B. 1983. *A history of pastoral care in America*. Nashville: Abingdon.

Holmes, U. 1980. *A history of Christian spirituality*. New York: Seabury.

Houston, J. 1984. Spirituality. In *The evangelical dictionary of theology*, ed. W. Elwell. Grand Rapids: Baker.

Ignatius of Loyola. 1964. *The spiritual exercises*. Trans. A. Mottola. New York: Image Books.

Jacobi, J. 1973. *The psychology of C. G. Jung*. New Haven: Yale University Press.

John of the Cross. 1964. *The collected works of St. John of the Cross*. Trans. K. Kavanaugh and O. Rodriguez. Garden City: Doubleday.

Jung, C. 1933. *Modern man in search of a soul*. New York: Harcourt, Brace, & Co.

———. 1936. Psychoanalysis and the cure of souls. In *The collected works of C. G. Jung*, ed. N. Read, M. Fordham, and G. Adler, vol. 11. Princeton: Princeton University Press.

168

————. 1961. *Memories dreams reflections.* New York: Pantheon Books.

————. 1975. *Letters, 2.* Princeton: Princeton University Press.

————. 1977. *The collected works of C. G. Jung,* ed. N. Read, M. Fordham, and G. Adler, vol. 11. Princeton: Princeton University Press.

Kelsey, M. 1968. *Dreams: The dark speech of the spirit.* New York: Doubleday.

Kierkegaard, S. 1954. *Fear and trembling and the sickness unto death.* Princeton: Princeton University Press.

Kopas, J. 1981. Jung and Assagioli in religious perspective. *Journal of Psychology and Theology* 9: 216–23.

Ladd, G. E. 1974. *A theology of the New Testament.* Grand Rapids: Eerdmans.

Laidlaw, J. 1895. *The Bible and the doctrine of man.* Edinburgh: T & T Clark.

Lambert, R., and M. Lambert. 1984. The effects of role preparation for psychotherapy on immigrant clients seeking mental health services in Hawaii. *The Journal of Community Psychology* 12: 263–75.

Lash, S. 1983. Orthodox spirituality. In *The Westminster dictionary of Christian spirituality,* ed. G. Wakefield. Philadelphia: Westminster.

Leech, K. 1977. *Soul friend.* San Francisco: Harper & Row.

Lovelace, R. 1979. *Dynamics of spiritual life.* Downers Grove: Inter-Varsity.

Luther, M. 1955. *Luther: Letters of spiritual counsel.* Ed. and trans. T. Tapert. Philadelphia: Westminster.

————. 1960. *Three treatises.* Philadelphia: Fortress.

————. 1968. A simple way to pray. In *Luther's Works,* ed. G. Wiencke, vol. 43. Philadelphia: Fortress.

McDonald, H. D. 1981. *The Christian view of man.* Westchester, Ill.: Good News.

MacKay, D. 1974. *The clock work image: A Christian perspective on science.* Downers Grove: Inter-Varsity.

McNamara, W. 1975. Psychology and the Christian mystical tradition. In *Transpersonal psychologies,* ed. C. Tart. New York: Harper & Row.

McNeill, J. T. 1951. *A history of the cure of souls.* New York: Harper & Row.

Malony, H. N., ed., 1980. *A Christian existential psychology: The contributions of John G. Finch.* Washington, D.C.: University Press of America.

Maruca, D. 1983. Roman Catholic spirituality. In *The Westminster dictionary of Christian spirituality,* ed. G. Wakefield. Philadelphia: Westminster.

Maslow, A. 1970. *Motivation and personality.* New York: Harper & Row.

May, G. 1982. *Will and spirit: A contemplative psychology.* San Francisco: Harper & Row.

Minirth, F. 1970. *Christian psychiatry*. Old Tappan: Revell.

Neaman, J. 1975. *Suggestions of the devil: The origins of madness*. New York: Anchor Books.

Needleman, J. 1975. *A sense of the cosmos*. Garden City: Doubleday.

Noll, M. 1984. Pietism. In *The evangelical dictionary of theology*, ed. W. Elwell. Grand Rapids: Baker.

Nordentoft, K. 1972. *Kierkegaard's psychology*. Pittsburgh: Dusquesne University Press.

Nouwen, H. 1966. *Reaching out*. Garden City: Doubleday.

Oden, T. C. 1972. *The intensive group experience: The new pietism*. Philadelphia: Westminster.

Otto, R. 1923. *The idea of the holy*. London: Oxford University Press.

Pannenberg, W. 1983. *Christian spirituality*. Philadelphia: Westminster.

Parloff, M., B. Iflund, and N. Goldstein. 1960. Communication of values and therapeutic change. *Archives of General Psychiatry* 2: 300–4.

Pattison, E. M. 1977. Psychosocial interpretations of exorcism. *Journal of Operational Psychiatry* 8: 5–21.

Pattison, E. M., and M. L. Pattison. 1980. Ex-gays: Religiously mediated change in homosexuals. *American Journal of Psychiatry* 137: 1553–62.

Richard, L. 1974. *The spirituality of John Calvin*. Atlanta: John Knox.

Rickel, W. 1954. Editorial. *Journal of Psychotherapy as a Religious Process* 1: 97.

Rieff, P. 1966. *The triumph of the therapeutic*. New York: Harper & Row.

Roberts, R. 1983. *Spirituality and human emotions*. Grand Rapids: Eerdmans.

Rosenthal, D. 1955. Changes in some moral values following psychotherapy. *Journal of Consulting Psychology* 19: 431–36.

Ryken, L. 1986. *Worldly saints: The Puritans as they really were*. Grand Rapids: Zondervan.

Sanford, J. 1968. *Dreams: God's forgotten language*. Philadelphia: Lippincott.

———, ed., 1984. *Fritz Kunkel: Selected writings*. New York: Paulist.

Sayers, D. 1941. *The mind of the Maker*. San Francisco: Harper & Row.

Solomon, C. 1971. *Handbook to happiness*. Wheaton: Tyndale.

Stoeffler, R. 1971. *The rise of evangelical pietism*. Leiden: E. J. Brill.

Strole, W., et al. 1962 *Mental health in the metropolis*. New York: McGraw-Hill.

Sugerman, S. 1976. *Sin and madness: Studies in narcissism*. Philadelphia: Westminster.

Szasz, T. 1961. *The myth of mental illness*. New York: Harper & Row.

———. 1978. *The myth of psychotherapy*. Garden City: Anchor.

Teresa of Avila. 1972. *Interior castle*. Trans. A. Peers. New York: Doubleday.

Tournier, P. 1963. *The strong and the weak*. Philadelphia: Westminster.

Tyrrell, B. J. 1982. *Christotherapy II*. New York: Paulist.

Vande Kemp, H. 1983. Spirit and soul in no-man's land: Reflections on Haule's "care of souls." *Journal of Psychology and Theology* 11: 117–22.

Vanderploeg, R. D. 1981. Imago Dei as foundational to psychotherapy: Integration versus segregation. *Journal of Psychology and Theology* 9: 299–304.

van Kaam, A. 1972. *On being yourself*. Denville, N.J.: Dimension Books.

Vitz, P. 1977. *Psychology as religion*. Grand Rapids: Eerdmans.

Wallace, E. 1983. Freud and religion: A history and reappraisal. In *The psychoanalytic study of society*, ed. L. Boyer, W. Muensterberger, and S. Grolnick, vol. 10. Hillsdale: Erlbaum.

Ware, K. 1974. *The power of the Name: The Jesus prayer in orthodox spirituality*. Oxford: SLG.

Watkins, O. 1972. *The Puritan experience: Studies in spiritual autobiography*. New York: Schocken Books.

Watson, J. 1930. *Introduction to behaviorism*. Chicago: University of Chicago Press.

Weaver, R. M. 1953. *The ethics of rhetoric*. Chicago: Regnery.

Werner, H. 1961. *Comparative psychology of mental development*. New York: Science Editions.

Witlock, G. 1960. The structure of personality in Hebrew psychology. *Interpretations* (January): 10–11.

Wolters, A. 1985. *Creation regained: Biblical basics for a reformational worldview*. Grand Rapids: Eerdmans.

Index